PAUL SIMON

LYRICS

1964 – 2011

SIMON & SCHUSTER PAPERBACKS
New York London Toronto Sydney New Delhi

SIMON & SCHUSTER PAPERBACKS
A Division of Simon & Schuster, Inc.
1230 Avenue of the Americas
New York, NY 10020

Copyright © 2008, 2011 by Paul Simon
Introduction copyright © 2008 by David Remnick
Foreword copyright © 2008 by Chuck Close
Lyrics compiled by Alan Light

This Simon & Schuster paperback edition September 2011

SIMON & SCHUSTER PAPERBACKS and colophon are registered
trademarks of Simon & Schuster, Inc.

For information about special discounts for bulk purchases,
please contact Simon & Schuster Special Sales at
1-800-456-6798 or business@simonandschuster.com.

Designed by Chip Kidd

Manufactured in the United States of America

10   9   8   7   6   5   4   3   2

The Library of Congress has cataloged the hardcover edition as follows:
Simon, Paul
[Songs. Texts]
    Lyrics 1964–2008 / Paul Simon.
        p.   cm.
    1. Songs—Texts.   I. Title.
ML54.6.S556L97   2008
782.42164'0268—dc22   2008014119

ISBN: 978-1-4516-4849-2
ISBN: 978-1-4165-9052-1 (ebook)

CONTENTS

v

1972 - 1977

1978 - 1983

ix

x

FOREWORD

If the experiences of people like me, who grew up in the 40s, 50s, and 60s, had been the subject of a movie, Paul Simon would have written the soundtrack of our lives. In fact, for the forty-plus years of my professional life as an artist, every single painting that I have executed has been painted with Paul's music playing in the background.

His music is appreciated by me, and probably the majority of his fans, just by letting his words and music wash over us as an experience—and what a powerful, rich, and varied experience that can be. Musicians, however, tell me that for those who share his musical craft, their appreciation is special. No less a composer than Philip Glass has called Paul the greatest songwriter of our time. Other musicians comment on his innovative rhythmic shifts, which are often abrupt and unexpected, and his unique use of chord changes and melodic transitions. He is univer-

sally admired by musicians of every stripe and every generation.

Artists are by nature generous in sharing their interest in and passion for the work of other artists of different generations and cultures. Think of Van Gogh and Japanese woodblock prints, Picasso and African tribal art, de Kooning and cubism, Warhol and advertising and pop culture. As an artist in a different medium, Paul shared his passion for doo-wop, R&B, and early rock and roll, and more famously went out of his culture to celebrate African, Caribbean, Latin American, and Cajun zydeco music, and the artists who invented those sounds. He has collaborated with other singer/songwriters, jazz and pop musicians, and vocalists of every stripe.

Paul and I have spoken often of our shared interest in "process," limitations, and innovation. We share many concerns, because the incremental nature of composing music with individual notes building larger units and phrases mirrors my process of constructing big, complicated images out of small, incremental passages of paint. He has recently shared with me his current process—starting with tapped rhythms, sometimes drumming with his fingers on the dashboard of his car while driving to Connecticut. These rhythmic shifts and changes suggest possible melodic options to fit that beat. Finally, that resultant sound—rhythm and melody together—will be wedded with lyrics that seem to him to "fit" the earlier layers of his process. This counterintuitive methodology is the opposite of his earliest technique, in which lyrics and melody came first, and makes clear how he has moved, changed, and evolved his process as he has matured as an artist. To keep all the balls in the air as styles change over forty years requires real effort and creativity. When the British invasion occurred, Paul was one of the few American musicians to weather the storm. In fact, his music had such authenticity and urgency for Americans that he was continuously played, going toe-to-toe with The Beatles and The Rolling Stones. He emerged from that competition with such power that many of his best recordings were made in the 80s and beyond. For me, *Graceland* represents the most perfect album ever recorded. Every song is a gem: varied, inventive, and divine.

In recent performances of his music at the Brooklyn Academy of Music, broken down into three bodies of work over as many nights, it became crystal clear what a national treasure Paul Simon has become, and just how right Philip Glass was—he is our greatest songwriter.

—**Chuck Close**

INTRODUCTION

Even at the peak of his popular stardom, Paul Simon was armed purely with his talent for the American song. He played arenas and stadiums, he had platinum records and made his fortune, but he was never magnificently cool like Lennon, darkly beautiful like Elvis, implacably enigmatic like Dylan, or three-quarters crazy like a hundred others. Style, roguishness, bad behavior, self-conscious unpredictability were never his tools. Modest in manner, he did not boast a mysterious background or invent one for himself. He came with less rock and roll packaging and tiresome self-invention than anyone in the business. And one effect of time has been to show how little the absence of theatricality mattered. Paul Simon's songs have become a part of life's fabric, an inner walking-around music. You stroll around New York and hear the echoes of his loneliness, his comedy, his passion, his ache, and his growing older. Even now, as he writes new songs and immerses

himself in yet another song form and rhythmic realm, he has secured his place in musical history. Simon stands with both the unpretentious masters of his own youth—the Everly Brothers, Chuck Berry, Smokey Robinson—and his greatest predecessors: Harold Arlen, Irving Berlin, Rodgers & Hart, the Gershwins, Johnny Mercer, and Cole Porter. As you browse through this book, the enormous (and unfinished) catalog of Paul Simon's art, you will see just how many songs he's written that rate with "How Deep Is the Ocean" and "Stormy Weather."

You undoubtedly know the story: Simon was born in Newark in 1941. He was raised in Kew Garden Hills, a middle-class area of Queens. His mother was an English teacher. His father was a professional bassist, but for a long time Paul had a limited interest in music. At a school production of *Alice in Wonderland* he became friends with Art Garfunkel—Paul was the White Rabbit, Art the Cheshire Cat—and, together

with two sisters, Angel and Ida Pel-
ligrini, they formed an a cappella
group and sang doo-wop songs.
Dispensing with the Pelligrinis,
the two boys performed as Tom
& Jerry and wrote an ebullient
pop song called "Hey Schoolgirl,"
which became a hit in 1957 for Big
Records. As teenagers they were
famous, appearing on a bill with
Jerry Lee Lewis on Dick Clark's
American Bandstand. In 1964, with
Dylan and The Beatles now in
full flower, and with college and
years of apprentice work now behind them, the two young men
re-formed in full ethnic name (a
rarity at the time) as Simon &
Garfunkel, with Paul providing the
songs and melodies and Art the
harmonies. Their first LP, *Wednesday Morning, 3 A.M.* featured "The
Sound of Silence," a number one
hit on the American charts.

Many of Simon's earliest songs
were the songs of a very young man,
full of longing and self-exploration.
The best of them—"The Sound
of Silence," "Homeward Bound,"
"America"—are tender, anthemic,
and inventive, but there was also a
quality in Simon's early work, often overlooked, of New York wit. It
was not the scornful and scabrous
finger-pointing style of "Don't
Think Twice, It's All Right" and "It
Ain't Me, Babe," but a wry, gentler
species of social comedy. In "The
Dangling Conversation," Simon
parodies a certain kind of wised-
up Manhattan conversation in
rapid quotation even as he ex-
presses his sense of lost love:

Yes, we speak of things that matter
With words that must be said
"Can analysis be worthwhile?"
"Is the theater really dead?"
And how the room has softly faded
And I only kiss your shadow
I cannot feel your hand
You're a stranger now unto me
Lost in the dangling conversation
And the superficial sighs
In the borders of our lives

What a book like this neglects,
unless you have a particularly acute
memory and encyclopedic ear, is
the musicality of the songs. The
danger of such a book is that it
seems to ask the reader to consider the lyrics as verse, written
for the page. But even the best
songs, Simon's included, are utterly linked to the melodic, har-

monic, and rhythmic qualities that go along with them. Simon was always a voracious consumer of songs and varieties of music—he would eventually combine forces with forms and players from New Orleans, Jamaica, Africa, Brazil, and elsewhere—but he was also a reader of English verse: W.B. Yeats, Wallace Stevens, Seamus Heaney, Philip Larkin, and, of course, his collaborator on *The Capeman*, Derek Walcott. He does not pretend to imitate those poets, but it is clear that he learned from them—their imagery and economy—as surely as he did from his musical forebears.

Take a song like "Duncan." Simon constructs a complicated narrative with incredible speed. Right away we get an autoportrait of the self-pitying boy in a cheap hotel room whose misery is compounded by the insatiably athletic couple in the next room ("Bound to win a prize"). We get his backstory in a few lines: the son of a fisherman and a "a fisherman's friend" ("And I was born in the boredom/And the chowder"). Penniless and on his own, he meets a preacher-girl, and, after the service, he creeps into her tent: "And my long years

of innocence ended." Now, as an older man, he remembers that awakening with pleasure and gratitude as he plays his guitar under the stars: "Just thanking the Lord/ For my fingers."

Although Simon first started writing hit songs in an era that had a tendency to mistake portentousness for meaning, his songs valued patient construction and a clear-as-gin transparency. This seems to be a conscious way of working for Simon. In 1990, when he was old enough to look back on his working method, he told an interviewer, Paul Zollo, "The easier it is for people to understand, the better it is, I think. As long as you're not sacrificing intelligence or insight or feeling in order to make it easier. If you can capture something that you feel is real and express it in a way that a lot of people can understand, that's rare and there's something about that that makes a piece have a certain kind of life. And if it enters into popular culture and it's not just about popular culture, then from a writer's point of view, that's a satisfying achievement."

Even as Simon's musical and

rhythmical goals became increasingly complex, particularly with the *Graceland* album, his lyrical strategy retained its determined patience. "You Can Call Me Al" begins like a "three-guys-walk-into-a-bar" gambit: "A man walks down the street." And he begins to ask himself why he is "soft in the middle" when the rest of his life is so hard. Simple as that: a man in the throes.

"You have to be a good host to people's attention span," Simon explained. "They're not going to come in there and work real hard right away. Too many things are coming: the music is coming, the rhythm is coming, all kinds of information that the brain is sorting out." In this song and many others, the more abstract or ornate images come later, but the listener is prepared because by now "those abstract images, they will just come down and fall into one of the slots that the mind has already made up about the structure of the song." A similar thing, with a different tactic, happens in the title song, "Graceland," which opens with a clear simile: "The Mississippi Delta/Was shining like a National

guitar." A National guitar, of course, is a steel-topped instrument that gleams like water. Two quick lines and we have entered a new world.

With time, many songs and their performers grow dated, as faintly ridiculous as an old fashion, a preposterous hat. We wonder, How could we have ever loved *that*? Simon's restless searching into himself, into forms of music undreamed of by the Everly Brothers, has been ambitious but always honest and unprepossessing. Maybe that is why Simon's best songs, whether sung by himself or by his most distinguished interpreters (think of Aretha Franklin on "Bridge Over Troubled Water"), do not date.

In the last pages of this book, you will encounter the songs of a writer no longer young, no longer at the top of the Billboard charts, but whose capacity for feeling and thought compressed into song has only deepened. In his maturity, he considers even the hardest thing with the serenity of the psalm writers. In "Quiet," Paul Simon is decades past youth, yet eager for the next chapter:

I am heading for a time of quiet
When my restlessness is past
And I can lie down on my
  blanket
And release my fists at last . . .
And I am heading for a place of
  quiet
Where the sage and sweet grass
  grow
By a lake of sacred water
From the mountain's melted
  snow.

—David Remnick
New York, New York

LYRICS

1964 – 2011

1964-1971

Wednesday Morning, 3 A.M.
Bleecker Street
Sparrow
The Sound of Silence
He Was My Brother
Wednesday Morning, 3 A.M.
Additional lyrics:
A Church Is Burning

Sounds of Silence
Leaves That Are Green
Blessed
Kathy's Song
Richard Cory
A Most Peculiar Man
April Come She Will
I Am a Rock
Additional lyrics:
Red Rubber Ball

Parsley, Sage, Rosemary and Thyme
Patterns
Cloudy
Homeward Bound
The Big Bright Green Pleasure
    Machine
The 59th Street Bridge Song
    (Feelin' Groovy)
The Dangling Conversation
Flowers Never Bend with the
    Rainfall
A Simple Desultory Philippic
    (or How I Was Robert
    McNamara'd Into Submission)

For Emily, Whenever I May Find Her
A Poem on the Underground Wall
7 O'Clock News/Silent Night

Bookends
Mrs. Robinson (from the motion
    picture *The Graduate*)
Save the Life of My Child
America
Overs
Old Friends
Bookends Theme
Fakin' It
Punky's Dilemma
A Hazy Shade of Winter
At the Zoo
Additional lyrics:
You Don't Know Where Your Interest Lies

Bridge Over Troubled Water
Bridge Over Troubled Water
El Condor Pasa (If I Could)
Cecilia
Keep the Customer Satisfied
So Long, Frank Lloyd Wright
The Boxer
Baby Driver
The Only Living Boy in New York
Why Don't You Write Me
Song for the Asking

WEDNESDAY MORNING, 3AM

exciting new sounds in the folk tradition by

SIMON & GARFUNKEL

Bleecker Street

Fog's rollin' in off the East River bank
Like a shroud, it covers Bleecker Street
Fills the alleys where men sleep
Hides the shepherd from the sheep

Voices leaking from a sad café
Smiling faces try to understand
I saw a shadow touch a shadow's hand
On Bleecker Street

A poet reads his crooked rhyme
Holy, holy is his sacrament
Thirty dollars pays your rent
On Bleecker Street

I heard a church bell softly chime
In a melody sustainin'
It's a long road to Canaan
On Bleecker Street
Bleecker Street

3

From the album *Wednesday Morning, 3 A.M.*

Sparrow

Who will love a little Sparrow
Who's traveled far and cries for rest?
"Not I," said the Oak Tree
"I won't share my branches with no sparrow's nest
And my blanket of leaves won't warm her cold breast"

Who will love a little Sparrow
And who will speak a kindly word?
"Not I," said the Swan
"The entire idea is utterly absurd
I'd be laughed at and scorned if the other Swans heard"

And who will take pity in his heart,
And who will feed a starving Sparrow?
"Not I," said the Golden Wheat
"I would if I could, but I cannot, I know
I need all my grain to prosper and grow"

Who will love a little Sparrow?
Will no one write her eulogy?
"I will," said the Earth
"For all I've created returns unto me
From dust were ye made and dust ye shall be"

From the album *Wednesday Morning, 3 A.M.*

Hello darkness, my old friend
I've come to talk with you again
Because a vision softly creeping
Left its seeds while I was sleeping
And the vision that was planted in my brain
Still remains
Within the sound of silence

In restless dreams I walked alone
Narrow streets of cobblestone
'Neath the halo of a streetlamp
I turned my collar to the cold and damp
When my eyes were stabbed by the flash of a neon light
That split the night
And touched the sound of silence

And in the naked light I saw
Ten thousand people, maybe more
People talking without speaking
People hearing without listening
People writing songs that voices never share
No one dare
Disturb the sound of silence

"Fools," said I, "You do not know
Silence like a cancer grows
Hear my words that I might teach you
Take my arms that I might reach you"
But my words like silent raindrops fell
And echoed in the wells of silence

And the people bowed and prayed
To the neon god they made
And the sign flashed out its warning
In the words that it was forming
And the sign said, "The words of the prophets
Are written on the subway walls
And tenement halls
And whispered in the sounds of silence"

From the album *Wednesday Morning, 3 A.M.*

He Was My Brother*

He was my brother
Five years older than I
He was my brother
Twenty-three years old the day he died

Freedom rider
They cursed my brother to his face
"Go home, outsider,
This town's gonna be your buryin' place"

He was singin' on his knees
An angry mob trailed along
They shot my brother dead
Because he hated what was wrong

He was my brother
Tears can't bring him back to me
He was my brother
And he died so his brothers could be free
He died so his brothers could be free

7

* for Andrew Goodman

From the album *Wednesday Morning, 3 A.M.*

Wednesday Morning, 3 A.M.

I can hear the soft breathing
Of the girl that I love
As she lies here beside me
Asleep with the night
And her hair, in a fine mist
Floats on my pillow
Reflecting the glow
Of the winter moonlight

She is soft, she is warm,
But my heart remains heavy
And I watch as her breasts
Gently rise, gently fall
For I know with the first light of dawn
I'll be leaving
And tonight will be
All I have left to recall

Oh, what have I done,
Why have I done it?
I've committed a crime,
I've broken the law
For twenty-five dollars
And pieces of silver
I held up and robbed
A hard liquor store

My life seems unreal,
My crime an illusion
A scene badly written
In which I must play
Yet I know as I gaze
At my young love beside me
The morning is just a few hours away

From the album *Wednesday Morning, 3 A.M.*

A Church Is Burning

A church is burning
The flames rise higher
Like hands that are praying, aglow in the sky
Like hands that are praying, the fire is saying
"You can burn down my churches, but I shall be free"

Three hooded men through the back roads did creep
Torches in their hands, while the village lies asleep
Down to the church, where just hours before
Voices were singing and hands were beating
And saying "I won't be a slave anymore"

And a church is burning
The flames rise higher
Like hands that are praying, aglow in the sky
Like hands that are praying, the fire is saying
"You can burn down my churches, but I shall be free"

Three hooded men, their hands lit the spark
Then they faded in the night, and they vanished in the dark
And in the cold light of morning, there's nothing that remains
But the ashes of a Bible and a can of kerosene

And a church is burning
The flames rise higher
Like hands that are praying, aglow in the sky
Like hands that are praying, the fire is saying
"You can burn down my churches, but I shall be free"

A church is more than just timber and stone
And freedom is a dark road when you're walking it alone
But the future is now, and it's time to take a stand
So the lost bells of freedom can ring out in my land

9

And a church is burning
The flames rise higher
Like hands that are praying, aglow in the sky
Like hands that are praying, the fire is saying
"You can burn down our churches, but I shall be free"

Leaves That Are Green

I was twenty-one years when I wrote this song
I'm twenty-two now, but I won't be for long
Time hurries on
And the leaves that are green turn to brown
And they wither with the wind
And they crumble in your hand

Once my heart was filled with the love of a girl
I held her close, but she faded in the night
Like a poem I meant to write
And the leaves that are green turned to brown
And they wither with the wind
And they crumble in your hand

I threw a pebble in a brook
And watched the ripples run away
And they never made a sound
And the leaves that are green turned to brown
And they wither with the wind
And they crumble in your hand
Hello, Hello, Hello, Hello,
Good-bye, Good-bye
Good-bye, Good-bye
That's all there is

And the leaves that are green turn to brown

From the album *Sounds of Silence*

13

Blessed

Blessed are the meek, for they shall inherit
Blessed is the lamb whose blood flows
Blessed are the sat upon, spat upon, ratted on
O Lord, Why have you forsaken me?
I got no place to go
I've walked around SoHo for the last night or so
Ah, but it doesn't matter, no

Blessed is the land and the kingdom
Blessed is the man whose soul belongs to
Blessed are the meth drinkers, pot sellers, illusion dwellers
O Lord, Why have you forsaken me?
My words trickle down from a wound
That I have no intention to heal

Blessed are the stained glass, windowpane glass
Blessed is the church service, makes me nervous
Blessed are the penny rookers, cheap hookers, groovy lookers
O Lord, Why have you forsaken me?
I have tended my own garden much too long

14

From the album *Sounds of Silence*

Kathy's Song

I hear the drizzle of the rain
Like a memory it falls
Soft and warm continuing
Tapping on my roof and walls

And from the shelter of my mind
Through the window of my eyes
I gaze beyond the rain-drenched streets
To England, where my heart lies

My mind's distracted and diffused
My thoughts are many miles away
They lie with you when you're asleep
And kiss you when you start your day

And a song I was writing is left undone
I don't know why I spend my time
Writing songs I can't believe
With words that tear and strain to rhyme

And so you see, I have come to doubt
All that I once held as true
I stand alone without beliefs
The only truth I know is you

And as I watch the drops of rain
Weave their weary paths and die
I know that I am like the rain
There but for the grace of you go I

From the album *Sounds of Silence*

15

They say that Richard Cory owns one-half of this whole town
With political connections to spread his wealth around
Born into society, a banker's only child
He had everything a man could want
Power, grace and style

But I work in his factory
And I curse the life I'm living
And I curse my poverty
And I wish that I could be
Oh, I wish that I could be
Oh, I wish that I could be
Richard Cory

The papers print his picture almost everywhere he goes
Richard Cory at the opera, Richard Cory at a show
And the rumor of his party and the orgies on his yacht!
Oh, he surely must be happy with everything he's got

But I, I work in his factory
And I curse the life I'm living
And I curse my poverty
And I wish that I could be
Oh, I wish that I could be
Oh, I wish that I could be
Richard Cory

He freely gave to charity, he had the common touch
And they were grateful for his patronage and they thanked him very
    much
So my mind was filled with wonder when the evening headlines read
"Richard Cory went home last night and put a bullet through his
    head"

But I, I work in his factory
And I curse the life I'm living
And I curse my poverty
And I wish that I could be
Oh, I wish that I could be
Oh, I wish that I could be
Richard Cory

From the album *Sounds of Silence*

17

He was A Most Peculiar Man
That's what Mrs. Riordan says, and she should know
She lived upstairs from him
She said he was a most peculiar man

He was A Most Peculiar Man
He lived all alone
Within a house, within a room, within himself
A Most Peculiar Man

He had no friends, he seldom spoke
And no one in turn ever spoke to him
'Cause he wasn't friendly and he didn't care
And he wasn't like them
Oh, no, he was A Most Peculiar Man

He died last Saturday
He turned on the gas and he went to sleep
With the windows closed so he'd never wake up
To his silent world and his tiny room

And Mrs. Riordan says he has a brother somewhere
Who should be notified soon
And all the people said
"What a shame that he's dead
But wasn't he A Most Peculiar Man?"

From the album *Sounds of Silence*

April Come She Will

April, come she will
When streams are ripe and swelled with rain
May, she will stay
Resting in my arms again

June, she'll change her tune
In restless walks, she'll prowl the night
July, she will fly
And give no warning to her flight

August, die she must
The autumn winds blow chilly and cold
September, I'll remember
A love once new has now grown old

From the album *Sounds of Silence*

19

I Am a Rock

A winter's day
In a deep and dark December
I am alone
Gazing from my window
To the streets below
On a freshly fallen, silent shroud of snow
I am a rock
I am an island

I've built walls
A fortress, steep and mighty
That none may penetrate
I have no need of friendship
Friendship causes pain
It's laughter and it's loving I disdain
I am a rock
I am an island

Don't talk of love
Well, I've heard the word before
It's sleeping in my memory
And I won't disturb the slumber
Of feelings that have died
If I never loved, I never would have cried
I am a rock
I am an island

I have my books
And my poetry to protect me
I am shielded in my armor
Hiding in my room
Safe within my womb
I touch no one and no one touches me
I am a rock
I am an island

And a rock feels no pain
And an island never cries

From the album *Sounds of Silence*

Red Rubber Ball

I should have known you'd bid me farewell
There's a lesson to be learned from this, and I learned it very well
Now, I know you're not the only starfish in the sea
If I never hear your name again, it's all the same to me

And I think it's gonna be alright
Yeah, the worst is over now
The mornin' sun is shinin' like a red rubber ball

You never care for secrets I confide
To you I'm just an ornament, somethin' for your pride
Always runnin', never carin', that's the life you live
Stolen minutes of your time were all you had to give

And I think it's gonna be alright
Yeah, the worst is over now
The mornin' sun is shinin' like a red rubber ball

The story's in the past with nothin' to recall
I've got my life to live, and I don't need you at all
The roller coaster ride we took is nearly at an end
I bought my ticket with my tears, that's all I'm gonna spend

And I think it's gonna be alright
Yeah, the worst is over now
The mornin' sun is shinin' like a red rubber ball

And I think it's gonna be alright
Yeah, the worst is over now
The mornin' sun is shinin' like a red rubber ball
It's bouncin' and it's shinin' like a red rubber ball

Patterns

The night sets softly
With the hush of falling leaves
Casting shivering shadows
On the houses through the trees
And the light from a streetlamp
Paints a pattern on my wall
Like the pieces of a puzzle
Or a child's uneven scrawl

Up a narrow flight of stairs
In a narrow little room
As I lie upon my bed
In the early evening gloom
Impaled on my wall
My eyes can dimly see
The pattern of my life
And the puzzle that is me

From the moment of my birth
To the instant of my death
There are patterns I must follow
Just as I must breathe each breath
Like a rat in a maze
The path before me lies
And the pattern never alters
Until the rat dies

The pattern still remains
On the wall where darkness fell
And it's fitting that it should
For in darkness I must dwell
Like the color of my skin
Or the day that I grow old
My life is made of patterns
That can scarcely be controlled

From the album *Parsley, Sage, Rosemary and Thyme*

25

Cloudy

Cloudy
The sky is gray and white and cloudy
Sometimes I think it's hanging down on me
And it's a hitchhike a hundred miles
I'm a ragamuffin child
Pointed finger-painted smile
I left my shadow waiting down the road for me a while

Cloudy
My thoughts are scattered and they're cloudy
They have no borders, no boundaries
They echo and they swell
From Tolstoy to Tinker Bell
Down from Berkeley to Carmel
Got some pictures in my pocket and a lot of time to kill

Hey, sunshine
I haven't seen you in a long time
Why don't you show your face and bend my mind?
These clouds stick to the sky
Like a floating question—why?
And they linger there to die
They don't know where they are going, and, my friend, neither do I

Cloudy
Cloudy

From the album *Parsley, Sage, Rosemary and Thyme*

Homeward Bound

I'm sittin' in the railway station
Got a ticket for my destination
On a tour of one-night stands
My suitcase and guitar in hand
And every stop is neatly planned
For a poet and a one-man band

Homeward bound
I wish I was
Homeward bound
Home, where my thought's escaping
Home, where my music's playing
Home, where my love lies waiting
Silently for me

Every day's an endless stream
Of cigarettes and magazines
And each town looks the same to me
The movies and the factories
And every stranger's face I see
Reminds me that I long to be

Homeward bound
I wish I was
Homeward bound
Home, where my thought's escaping
Home, where my music's playing
Home, where my love lies waiting
Silently for me

Tonight I'll sing my songs again
I'll play the game and pretend
But all my words come back to me
In shades of mediocrity
Like emptiness in harmony
I need someone to comfort me

Homeward bound
I wish I was
Homeward bound
Home, where my thought's escaping
Home, where my music's playing
Home, where my love lies waiting
Silently for me
Silently for me

From the album *Parsley, Sage, Rosemary and Thyme*

Do people have a tendency to dump on you?
Does your group have more cavities than theirs?
Do all the hippies seem to get the jump on you?
Do you sleep alone when others sleep in pairs?
Well, there's no need to complain
We'll eliminate your pain
We can neutralize your brain
You'll feel just fine
Now
Buy a big bright green pleasure machine!

Do figures of authority just shoot you down?
Is life within the business world a drag?
Did your boss just mention that you'd better shop around
To find yourself a more productive bag?
Are you worried and distressed?
Can't seem to get no rest?
Put our product to the test
You'll feel just fine
Now
Buy a big bright green pleasure machine!

29

You'd better hurry up and order one
Our limited supply is very nearly gone

Do you nervously await the blows of cruel fate?
Do your checks bounce higher than a rubber ball?
Are you worried 'cause your girlfriend's just a little late?
Are you looking for a way to chuck it all?
We can end your daily strife
At a reasonable price
You've seen it advertised in Life
You'll feel just fine
Now
Buy a big bright green pleasure machine!

From the album *Parsley, Sage, Rosemary and Thyme*

The 59th Street Bridge Song (Feelin' Groovy)

Slow down, you move too fast
You got to make the morning last
Just kicking down the cobblestones
Looking for fun and feelin' groovy
Ba da da da da da da, feelin' groovy

Hello, lamppost, what'cha knowin'?
I've come to watch your flowers growin'
Ain't cha got no rhymes for me?
Doot-in doo-doo, feelin' groovy
Ba da da da da da da, feelin' groovy

I got no deeds to do
No promises to keep
I'm dappled and drowsy and ready to sleep
Let the morning time drop all its petals on me
Life, I love you
All is groovy

From the album *Parsley, Sage, Rosemary and Thyme*

The Dangling Conversation

It's a still-life watercolor
Of a now late afternoon
As the sun shines through the curtain lace
And shadows wash the room
And we sit and drink our coffee
Couched in our indifference
Like shells upon the shore
You can hear the ocean roar
In the dangling conversation
And the superficial sighs
The borders of our lives

And you read your Emily Dickinson
And I my Robert Frost
And we note our place with bookmarkers
That measure what we've lost
Like a poem poorly written
We are verses out of rhythm
Couplets out of rhyme
In syncopated time
And the dangling conversation
And the superficial sighs
Are the borders of our lives

Yes, we speak of things that matter
With words that must be said
"Can analysis be worthwhile?"
"Is the theater really dead?"
And how the room has softly faded
And I only kiss your shadow
I cannot feel your hand
You're a stranger now unto me
Lost in the dangling conversation
And the superficial sighs
In the borders of our lives

From the album *Parsley, Sage, Rosemary and Thyme*

Through the corridors of sleep
Past shadows, dark and deep
My mind dances and leaps in confusion
I don't know what is real
I can't touch what I feel
And I hide behind the shield of my illusion

So I'll continue to continue to pretend
My life will never end
And flowers never bend
With the rainfall

The mirror on my wall
Casts an image dark and small
But I'm not sure at all it's my reflection
I am blinded by the light
Of God and truth and right
And I wander in the night without direction

So I'll continue to continue to pretend
My life will never end
And flowers never bend
With the rainfall

No matter if you're born
To play the king or pawn
For the line is thinly drawn 'tween joy and sorrow
So my fantasy
Becomes reality
And I must be what I must be and face tomorrow

So I'll continue to continue to pretend
My life will never end
And flowers never bend
With the rainfall

From the album *Parsley, Sage, Rosemary and Thyme*

32

A Simple Desultory Philippic (or How I Was Robert McNamara'd Into Submission)

I been Norman Mailered, Maxwell Taylored
I been John O'Hara'd, McNamara'd
I been Rolling Stoned and Beatled till I'm blind
I been Ayn Randed, nearly branded
A Communist, 'cause I'm left-handed
That's the hand I use, well, never mind!

I been Phil Spectored, resurrected
I been Lou Adlered, Barry Sadlered
Well, I paid all the dues I want to pay
And I learned the truth from Lenny Bruce
And all my wealth won't buy me health
So I smoke a pint of tea a day

I knew a man, his brain so small
He couldn't think of nothing at all
He's not the same as you and me
He doesn't dig poetry
He's so unhip
When you say Dylan, he thinks you're talking about Dylan Thomas
Whoever he was
The man ain't got no culture
But it's alright, ma
Everybody must get stoned

I been Mick Jaggered, silver daggered
Andy Warhol, won't you please come home?
I been mothered, fathered, aunt and uncled
Been Roy Haleed and Art Garfunkeled
I just discovered somebody's tapped my phone

From the album *Parsley, Sage, Rosemary and Thyme*

For Emily, Whenever I May Find Her

What a dream I had
Pressed in organdy
Clothed in crinoline of smoky burgundy
Softer than the rain
I wandered empty streets
Down past the shop displays
I heard cathedral bells
Tripping down the alleyways
As I walked on

And when you ran to me
Your cheeks flushed with the night
We walked on frosted fields
Of juniper and lamplight
I held your hand

And when I awoke and felt you warm and near
I kissed your honey hair with my grateful tears
Oh, I love you, girl
Oh, I love you

34

From the album *Parsley, Sage, Rosemary and Thyme*

The last train is nearly due
The underground is closing soon
And in the dark deserted station
Restless in anticipation
A man waits in the shadows

His restless eyes leap and scratch
At all that they can touch or catch
And hidden deep within his pocket
Safe within its silent socket
He holds a colored crayon

Now from the tunnel's stony womb
The carriage rides to meet the groom
And opens wide and welcome doors
But he hesitates, then withdraws
Deeper in the shadows

And the train is gone suddenly
On wheels clicking silently
Like a gently tapping litany
And he holds his crayon rosary
Tighter in his hand

35

Now from his pocket quick he flashes
The crayon on the wall he slashes
Deep upon the advertising
A single-worded poem comprised
Of four letters

And his heart is laughing, screaming, pounding
The poem across the tracks rebounding
Shadowed by the exit light
His legs take their ascending flight
To seek the breast of darkness and be suckled by the night

From the album *Parsley, Sage, Rosemary and Thyme*

Silent night, holy night
All is calm, all is bright
Round yon Virgin mother and child
Holy infant, so tender and mild
Sleep in heavenly peace
Sleep in heavenly peace

. . . Brought traditional enemies together, but left the defenders of
the measure without the votes of their strongest supporters.
President Johnson originally proposed an outright ban covering
discrimination by everyone for every type of housing, but it had no
chance from the start and everyone in Congress knew it.
A compromise was painfully worked out in the House Judiciary
Committee.

In Los Angeles today comedian Lenny Bruce died of what was
believed to be an overdose of narcotics.
Bruce was forty-two years old.

Dr. Martin Luther King says he does not intend to cancel plans for an
open housing march Sunday in the Chicago suburbs of Cicero.
Cook County Sheriff Richard Ogilvie asked King to call off the
march, and the police in Cicero said they would ask the National
Guard be called out if it is held.
King, now in Atlanta, Georgia, plans to return to Chicago Tuesday.

In Chicago Richard Speck, accused murderer of nine student nurses,
was brought before a grand jury today for indictment.
The nurses were found stabbed and strangled in their Chicago
apartment.

In Washington the atmosphere was tense today as a special
   subcommittee of the House Committee on Un-American
   Activities continued its probe into anti–Vietnam War protest.
Demonstrators were forcibly evicted from the hearings when they
   began chanting antiwar slogans.

Former vice president Richard Nixon says that unless there is a
   substantial increase in the present war effort in Vietnam, the U.S.
   should look forward to five more years of war.
In a speech before the Convention of the Veterans of Foreign Wars in
   New York, Nixon also said opposition to the war in this country is
   the greatest single weapon working against the U.S.

That's the 7 o'clock edition of the news. Good-night.

Silent night, holy night
All is calm, all is bright
Round yon Virgin mother and child
Holy infant, so tender and mild
Sleep in heavenly peace
Sleep in heavenly peace

37

From the album *Parsley, Sage, Rosemary and Thyme*

BOOKENDS/SIMON & GARFUNKEL

Mrs. Robinson

(from the motion picture *The Graduate*)

And here's to you, Mrs. Robinson
Jesus loves you more than you will know, wo wo wo
God bless you please, Mrs. Robinson
Heaven holds a place for those who pray, hey hey hey
Hey hey hey

We'd like to know a little bit about you for our files
We'd like to help you learn to help yourself
Look around you, all you see are sympathetic eyes
Stroll around the grounds until you feel at home

And here's to you, Mrs. Robinson
Jesus loves you more than you will know, wo wo wo
God bless you please, Mrs. Robinson
Heaven holds a place for those who pray, hey hey hey
Hey hey hey

Hide it in a hiding place where no one ever goes
Put it in your pantry with your cupcakes
It's a little secret, just the Robinsons' affair
Most of all, you've got to hide it from the kids

Coo coo ca-choo, Mrs. Robinson
Jesus loves you more than you will know, wo wo wo
God bless you please, Mrs. Robinson
Heaven holds a place for those who pray, hey hey hey
Hey hey hey

Sitting on a sofa on a Sunday afternoon
Going to the candidates' debate
Laugh about it, shout about it
When you've got to choose
Every way you look at it you lose

Where have you gone, Joe DiMaggio?
A nation turns its lonely eyes to you, woo woo woo
What's that you say, Mrs. Robinson?
"Joltin' Joe" has left and gone away, hey hey hey
Hey hey hey

From the album *Bookends*

40

Save the Life of My Child

"Good God! Don't jump!"
A boy sat on the ledge
An old man who had fainted was revived
And everyone agreed 'twould be a miracle indeed
If the boy survived
"Save the life of my child!"
Cried the desperate mother

The woman from the supermarket
Ran to call the cops
"He must be high on something," someone said
Though it never made the *New York Times*
In the *Daily News*, the caption read
"Save the life of my child!"
Cried the desperate mother

A patrol car passing by
Halted to a stop
Said Officer MacDougal in dismay
"The force can't do a decent job
'Cause the kids got no respect
For the law today" (and blah blah blah)
"Save the life of my child!"
Cried the desperate mother
"Oh, what's becoming of the children?"
People asking each other

When darkness fell, excitement kissed the crowd
And it made them wild
In the atmosphere of freaky holiday
When the spotlight hit the boy
And the crowd began to cheer
He flew away

"Oh, my Grace, I got no hiding place"
"Oh, my Grace, I got no hiding place"

From the album *Bookends*

41

America

"Let us be lovers, we'll marry our fortunes together
I've got some real estate here in my bag"
So we bought a pack of cigarettes and Mrs. Wagner's pies
And walked off to look for America

"Kathy," I said, as we boarded a Greyhound in Pittsburgh
"Michigan seems like a dream to me now
It took me four days to hitchhike from Saginaw
I've come to look for America"

Laughing on the bus
Playing games with the faces
She said the man in the gabardine suit was a spy
I said, "Be careful, his bow tie is really a camera"

"Toss me a cigarette, I think there's one in my raincoat"
"We smoked the last one an hour ago"
So I looked at the scenery, she read her magazine
And the moon rose over an open field

"Kathy, I'm lost," I said, though I knew she was sleeping
"I'm empty and aching and I don't know why"
Counting the cars on the New Jersey Turnpike
They've all come to look for America
All come to look for America
All come to look for America

From the album Bookends

Why don't we stop fooling ourselves?
The game is over, over, over
No good times, no bad times
There's no times at all
Just the *New York Times*
Sitting on the windowsill
Near the flowers

We might as well be apart
It hardly matters
We sleep separately
And drop a smile passing in the hall
But there's no laughs left
'Cause we laughed them all
And we laughed them all
In a very short time

Time
Is tapping on my forehead
Hanging from my mirror
Rattling the teacups
And I wonder

How long can I delay?
We're just a habit
Like saccharin
And I'm habitually feelin' kinda blue
But each time I try on
The thought of leaving you
I stop . . .
I stop and think it over

43

From the album *Bookends*

Old Friends

Old friends
Old friends
Sat on their park bench
Like bookends
A newspaper blown through the grass
Falls on the round toes
Of the high shoes
Of the old friends

Old friends
Winter companions
The old men
Lost in their overcoats
Waiting for the sunset
The sounds of the city
Sifting through trees
Settle like dust
On the shoulders
Of the old friends

44

Can you imagine us
Years from today
Sharing a park bench quietly?
How terribly strange
To be seventy

Old friends
Memory brushes the same years
Silently sharing the same fear

From the album *Bookends*

Bookends Theme

Time it was,
And what a time it was
It was . . .
A time of innocence
A time of confidences

Long ago . . . it must be . . .
I have a photograph
Preserve your memories
They're all that's left you

From the album *Bookends*

45

When she goes, she's gone
If she stays, she stays here
The girl does what she wants to do
She knows what she wants to do
And I know I'm fakin' it
I'm not really makin' it

I'm such a dubious soul
And a walk in the garden
Wears me down
Tangled in the fallen vines
Pickin' up the punch lines
I've just been fakin' it
Not really makin' it
No, no, no

Is there any danger?
No, no, not really
Just lean on me
Takin' time to treat
Your friendly neighbors honestly
I've just been fakin' it
Not really makin' it
This feeling of fakin' it
I still haven't shaken it

Prior to this lifetime
I surely was a tailor
Look at me
("Good morning, Mr. Leitch.
Have you had a busy day?")
I own the tailor's face and hands
I am the tailor's face and hands
I know I'm fakin' it, fakin' it
I'm not really makin' it
This feeling of fakin' it
I still haven't shaken it, shaken it
I know I'm fakin' it
I'm not really makin' it

From the album *Bookends*

Punky's Dilemma

Wish I was a Kellogg's Cornflake
Floatin' in my bowl takin' movies
Relaxin' awhile, livin' in style
Talkin' to a raisin who occasionally plays L.A.
Casually glancing at his toupee

Wish I was an English muffin
'Bout to make the most out of a toaster
I'd ease myself down
Comin' up brown
I prefer boysenberry
More than any ordinary jam
I'm a "Citizens for Boysenberry Jam" fan

Ah, South California

If I become a first lieutenant
Would you put my photo on your piano?
"To Maryjane—
Best wishes, Martin"

Old Roger draft dodger
Leavin' by the basement door
Everybody knows what he's
Tippy-toeing down there for

From the album *Bookends*

48

Time, time, time
See what's become of me
While I looked around for my possibilities
I was so hard to please
But look around
Leaves are brown
And the sky is a hazy shade of winter

Hear the Salvation Army band
Down by the riverside's
Bound to be a better ride
Than what you've got planned
Carry your cup in your hand
And look around you
Leaves are brown, now
And the sky is a hazy shade of winter

Hang on to your hopes, my friend
That's an easy thing to say
But if your hopes should pass away
Simply pretend
That you can build them again
Look around
The grass is high
The fields are ripe
It's the springtime of my life

Seasons change with the scenery
Weaving time in a tapestry
Won't you stop and remember me
At any convenient time?
Funny how my memory skips
While looking over manuscripts
Of unpublished rhyme
Drinking my vodka and lime
I look around
Leaves are brown, now
And the sky is a hazy shade of winter
Look around
Leaves are brown
There's a patch of snow on the ground
Look around
Leaves are brown
There's a patch of snow on the ground

From the album *Bookends*

At the Zoo

Someone told me
It's all happening at the zoo
I do believe it
I do believe it's true

It's a light and tumble journey
From the East Side to the park
Just a fine and fancy ramble to the zoo
But you can take a crosstown bus
If it's raining or it's cold
And the animals will love it if you do
If you do, now

Somethin' tells me
It's all happening at the zoo
I do believe it
I do believe it's true

The monkeys stand for honesty
Giraffes are insincere
And the elephants are kindly, but they're dumb
Orangutans are skeptical
Of changes in their cages
And the zookeeper is very fond of rum

Zebras are reactionaries
Antelopes are missionaries
Pigeons plot in secrecy
And hamsters turn on frequently
What a gas!
You gotta come and see
At the zoo
At the zoo

From the album *Bookends*

51

You Don't Know Where Your Interest Lies

You don't know that you love me
You don't know, but I know that you do
You may think you're above me, yeah
What you think isn't always true

Don't try to debate me
You should know that I'm womanly wise
Still, you try to manipulate me
You don't know where your interest lies
No, you don't know where your interest lies
You don't begin to comprehend

You're just a game that I like to play
You may think that we're friends, all right
But I won't let friendship get in my way
No, I won't let friendship get in my way

Indications indicate
Runnin' the same riff will turn you around
Obviously, you're going to blow it
But you don't know it

52

You don't know that you love me
You don't know, but I know that you do
You may think you're above me, yeah
What you think isn't always true
And you don't know where your interest lies
You don't know where your interest lies

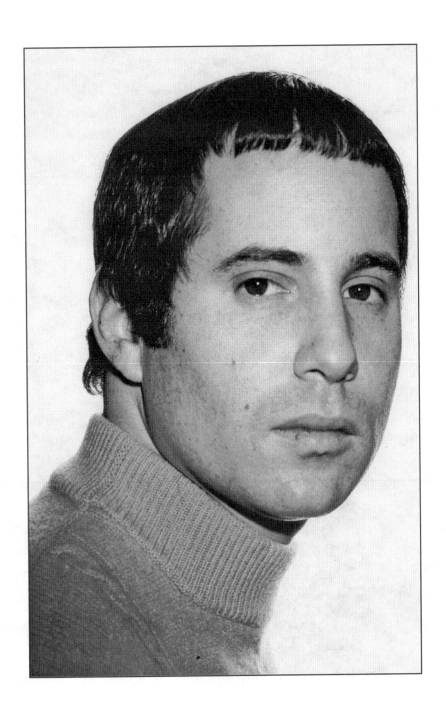

Simon
and
Garfunkel
Bridge
Over
Troubled
Water

Bridge Over Troubled Water

When you're weary, feeling small
When tears are in your eyes
I will dry them all
I'm on your side
When times get rough
And friends just can't be found
Like a bridge over troubled water
I will lay me down
Like a bridge over troubled water
I will lay me down

When you're down and out
When you're on the street
When evening falls so hard
I will comfort you
I'll take your part
When darkness comes
And pain is all around
Like a bridge over troubled water
I will lay me down
Like a bridge over troubled water
I will lay me down

Sail on, silvergirl
Sail on by
Your time has come to shine
All your dreams are on their way
See how they shine
If you need a friend
I'm sailing right behind
Like a bridge over troubled water
I will ease your mind
Like a bridge over troubled water
I will easc your mind

From the album *Bridge Over Troubled Water*

El Condor Pasa (If I Could)

I'd rather be a sparrow than a snail
Yes, I would
If I could
I surely would

I'd rather be a hammer than a nail
Yes, I would
If I only could
I surely would

Away, I'd rather sail away
Like a swan that's here and gone
A man gets tied up to the ground
He gives the world its saddest sound
Its saddest sound

I'd rather be a forest than a street
Yes, I would
If I could
I surely would

56

I'd rather feel the earth beneath my feet
Yes, I would
If I only could
I surely would

From the album *Bridge Over Troubled Water*

Cecilia

Celia, you're breaking my heart
You're shaking my confidence daily
Oh, Cecilia, I'm down on my knees
I'm begging you please to come home
Celia, you're breaking my heart
You're shaking my confidence daily
Oh, Cecilia, I'm down on my knees
I'm begging you please to come home
Come on home

Making love in the afternoon
With Cecilia
Up in my bedroom
I got up to wash my face
When I come back to bed
Someone's taken my place

Celia, you're breaking my heart
You're shaking my confidence daily
Oh, Cecilia, I'm down on my knees
I'm begging you please to come home
Come on home

Jubilation
She loves me again
I fall on the floor and I laughing
Jubilation,
She loves me again
I fall on the floor and I laughing

From the album *Bridge Over Troubled Water*

Gee, but it's great to be back home
Home is where I want to be
I've been on the road so long, my friend
And if you came along
I know you couldn't disagree
It's the same old story, yeah
Everywhere I go
I get slandered, libeled
I hear words I never heard in the Bible
And I'm one step ahead of the shoe shine
Two steps away from the county line
Just trying to keep my customers satisfied
Satisfied

Deputy Sheriff said to me
"Tell me what you come here for, boy
You better get your bags and flee
You're in trouble, boy
And now you're heading into more"
It's the same old story
Everywhere I go
I get slandered, libeled
I hear words I never heard in the Bible
And I'm one step ahead of the shoe shine
Two steps away from the county line
Just trying to keep my customers satisfied
Satisfied

58

And it's the same old story
Everywhere I go
I get slandered, libeled
I hear words I never heard in the Bible
And I'm so tired
I'm oh, so tired
But I'm trying to keep my customers satisfied
Satisfied

From the album *Bridge Over Troubled Water*

So long, Frank Lloyd Wright
I can't believe your song is gone so soon
I barely learned the tune
So soon
So soon

I'll remember Frank Lloyd Wright
All of the nights we'd harmonize till dawn
I never laughed so long
So long
So long

Architects may come and
Architects may go and
Never change your point of view
When I run dry
I stop a while and think of you

So long, Frank Lloyd Wright
All of the nights we'd harmonize till dawn
I never laughed so long
So long
So long

60

From the album *Bridge Over Troubled Water*

The Boxer

I am just a poor boy
Though my story's seldom told
I have squandered my resistance
For a pocketful of mumbles
Such are promises
All lies and jests
Still, a man hears what he wants to hear
And disregards the rest

When I left my home and my family
I was no more than a boy
In the company of strangers
In the quiet of the railway station
Running scared
Laying low, seeking out the poorer quarters
Where the ragged people go
Looking for the places only they would know
Lie-la-lie . . .

Asking only workman's wages
I come looking for a job
But I get no offers
Just a come-on from the whores on Seventh Avenue
I do declare, there were times when I was so lonesome
I took some comfort there
Lie-la-lie . . .

Now the years are rolling by me
They are rocking easily
I am older than I once was
And younger than I'll be
But that's not unusual
No, it isn't strange
After changes upon changes
We are more or less the same
After changes we are
More or less the same

Then I'm laying out my winter clothes
And wishing I was gone
Going home
Where the New York City winters aren't bleeding me
Leading me
Going home

In the clearing stands a boxer
And a fighter by his trade
And he carries the reminders
Of every glove that laid him down
Or cut him till he cried out
In his anger and his shame
"I am leaving, I am leaving"
But the fighter still remains
Lie-la-lie . . .

62

From the album *Bridge Over Troubled Water*

My daddy was the family bassman
My mamma was an engineer
And I was born one dark gray morn
With music humming in my ears
In my ears

They call me Baby Driver
And once upon a pair of wheels
Hit the road and I'm gone
What's my number?
I wonder how your engines feel

Ba ba ba ba
Scoot down the road
What's my number?
I wonder how your engines feel
Shine the light

My daddy was a prominent frogman
My mamma's in the Naval Reserve
When I was young, I carried a gun
But I never got the chance to serve
I did not serve

They call me Baby Driver
And once upon a pair of wheels
Hit the road and I'm gone
What's my number?
I wonder how your engines feel

Ba ba ba ba
Scoot down the road
What's my number?
I wonder how your engines feel

63

My daddy got a big promotion
My mamma got a raise in pay
There's no one home, we're all alone
Oh, come into my room and play
Yes, we can play

I'm not talking about your pigtails
But I'm talking 'bout your sex appeal
Hit the road and I'm gone
What's my number?
I wonder how your engines feel
Ba ba ba ba
Scoot down the road
What's my number?
I wonder how your engines feel

From the album *Bridge Over Troubled Water*

64

Tom, get your plane right on time
I know your part'll go fine
Fly down to Mexico
Da-n-da-da-n-da-n-da-da and here I am
The only living boy in New York

I get the news I need on the weather report
Oh, I can gather all the news I need on the weather report
Hey, I've got nothing to do today but smile
Da-n-da-da-n-da-n-da-da and here I am
The only living boy in New York

Half of the time we're gone, but we don't know where
And we don't know where
Here I am
Half of the time we're gone, but we don't know where
And we don't know where

Tom, get your plane right on time
I know that you've been eager to fly now
Hey, let your honesty shine, shine, shine
Like it shines on me
The only living boy in New York
The only living boy in New York

65

From the album *Bridge Over Troubled Water*

Why don't you write me?
I'm out in the jungle
I'm hungry to hear you
Send me a card
I am waiting so hard
To be near you

Why don't you write?
Something is wrong
And I know I got to be there
Maybe I'm lost
But I can't make the cost
Of the airfare

Tell me why, why, why
Tell me why, why, why

Why don't you write me?
A letter would brighten
My loneliest evening
Mail it today
If it's only to say
That you're leaving me

Monday morning, sitting in the sun
Hoping and wishing for the mail to come
Tuesday, never got a word
Wednesday, Thursday, ain't no sign
Drank half a bottle of iodine
Friday, woe is me
I'm gonna hang my body from the highest tree
Why don't you write me?
Why don't you write me?

From the album *Bridge Over Troubled Water*

Song for the Asking

Here is my song for the asking
Ask me and I will play
So sweetly, I'll make you smile

This is my tune for the taking
Take it, don't turn away
I've been waiting all my life

Thinking it over, I've been sad
Thinking it over, I'd be more than glad
To change my ways for the asking
Ask me and I will play
All the love that I hold inside

From the album *Bridge Over Troubled Water*

1972-1977

Paul Simon
Mother and Child Reunion
Duncan
Everything Put Together Falls
    Apart
Run That Body Down
Armistice Day
Me and Julio Down by the
    Schoolyard
Peace Like a River
Papa Hobo
Paranoia Blues
Congratulations

There Goes Rhymin' Simon
Kodachrome
Tenderness
Take Me to the Mardi Gras
Something So Right
One Man's Ceiling Is Another
    Man's Floor

American Tune
Was a Sunny Day
Learn How to Fall
St. Judy's Comet
Loves Me Like a Rock

Still Crazy After All These Years
Still Crazy After All These Years
My Little Town
I Do It for Your Love
50 Ways to Leave Your Lover
Night Game
Gone at Last
Some Folks' Lives Roll Easy
Have a Good Time
You're Kind
Silent Eyes

Additional lyrics:
Stranded in a Limousine
Slip Slidin' Away

PAUL
SIMON

UPTEMPO

FADE

5   MOTHER AND CHILD REUNION   (3:00)

NO I WOULD NOT GIVE YOU FALSE HOPE
ON THIS STRANGE AND MOURNFUL DAY
BUT THE MOTHER AND CHILD REUNION
IS ONLY A MOTION AWAY

I CAN'T FOR THE LIFE OF ME
REMEMBER A ~~SADDER~~ DAY
I KNOW THEY SAY LET IT BE
BUT IT JUST DON'T WORK OUT THAT WAY
AND THE COURSE OF A LIFETIME RUNS
OVER AND OVER AGAIN

I JUST CAN'T BELIEVE IT'S SO
~~AND I KNOW THOUGH~~ IT SEEMS STRANGE TO SAY
BUT I NEVER BEEN LAID SO LOW .
IN SUCH A MYSTERIOUS WAY
AND THE COURSE OF A LIFETIME RUNS
OVER AND OVER AGAIN

BUT I WOULD NOT GIVE YOU FALSE HOPE
ON THIS STRANGE AND MOURNFUL DAY
~~WHEN~~ THE MOTHER AND CHILD REUNION
IS ONLY A MOTION AWAY

No, I would not give you false hope
On this strange and mournful day
But the mother and child reunion
Is only a motion away
Oh, little darling of mine

I can't for the life of me
Remember a sadder day
I know they say let it be
But it just don't work out that way
And the course of a lifetime runs
Over and over again

No, I would not give you false hope
On this strange and mournful day
But the mother and child reunion
Is only a motion away
Oh, little darling of mine

I just can't believe it's so
Though it seems strange to say
I never been laid so low
In such a mysterious way
And the course of a lifetime runs
Over and over again

But I would not give you false hope
On this strange and mournful day
When the mother and child reunion
Is only a motion away

Oh, the mother and child reunion
Is only a motion away
Oh, the mother and child reunion
Is only a moment away

From the album *Paul Simon*

Couple in the next room
Bound to win a prize
They've been going at it all night long
Well, I'm trying to get some sleep
But these motel walls are cheap
Lincoln Duncan is my name
And here's my song, here's my song

My father was a fisherman
My mama was a fisherman's friend
And I was born in the boredom
And the chowder
So when I reached my prime
I left my home in the Maritimes
Headed down the turnpike for
New England, sweet New England

Holes in my confidence
Holes in the knees of my jeans
I was left without a penny in my pocket
Oo-we, I was destituted
As a kid could be
And I wished I wore a ring
So I could hock, I'd like to hock it

A young girl in a parking lot
Was preaching to a crowd
Singing sacred songs and reading
From the Bible
Well, I told her I was lost
And she told me all about the Pentecost
And I seen that girl as the road
To my survival

Just later on the very same night
I crept to her tent with a flashlight
And my long years of innocence ended
Well, she took me to the woods
Saying here comes something and it feels so good
And just like a dog I was befriended
I was befriended

Oh, oh, what a night
Oh, what a garden of delight
Even now that sweet memory lingers
I was playing my guitar
Lying underneath the stars
Just thanking the Lord
For my fingers
For my fingers

From the album *Paul Simon*

Paraphernalia
Never hides your broken bones
And I don't know why
You'd want to try
It's plain to see you're on your own
Oh, I ain't blind, no
Some folks are crazy
Others walk that borderline
Watch what you're doing

Taking downs to get off to sleep
And ups to start you on your way
After a while, they'll change your style
I see it happening every day
Oh, spare your heart
Everything put together
Sooner or later falls apart

There's nothing to it, nothing to it
You can cry
And you can lie
For all the good it'll do you
You can die
But when it's done
The police come, and they lay you down for dead
Oh, just remember what I said

75

From the album *Paul Simon*

Went to my doctor yesterday
She said I seem to be okay
She said, "Paul, you better look around
How long you think that you can
Run that body down?
How many nights you think that you can
Do what you been doin'?
Who, now who you foolin'?"

I came back home and I went to bed
I was resting my head
My wife came in and she said
"What's wrong, sweet boy, what's wrong?"
I told her what's wrong
I said, "Peg, you better look around
How long you think that you can
Run that body down?
How many nights you think that you can
Do what you been doin'?
Now who you foolin'?
Who you foolin'?
Who you foolin'?"

Kid, you better look around
How long you think that you can
Run that body down?
How many nights you think that you can
Do what you been doin'?
Who, now who you foolin'?
Who you foolin'?
Who you foolin'?

From the album *Paul Simon*

Armistice Day

On Armistice Day
The Philharmonic will play
But the songs that we sing
Will be sad
Shufflin' brown tunes
Hanging around

No long-drawn, blown-out excuses
Were made
When I needed a friend, she was there
Just like an easy chair

Armistice Day
Armistice Day
That's all I really wanted to say

Oh, I'm weary from waiting
In Washington, DC
I'm coming to see my congressman
But he's avoiding me
Weary from waiting down in Washington, DC

Oh, Congresswoman
Won't you tell that congressman
I've waited such a long time
I've about waited all I can
Oh, Congresswoman
Won't you tell that congressman

From the album *Paul Simon*

UNTEMED

FADE

(3:10)

4 ME AND JULIO DOWN BY THE SCHOOLYARD

THE MAMA PAJAMA ROLLED OUT OF BED
AND SHE RAN TO THE POLICE STATION
WHEN THE PAPA FOUND OUT HE BEGAN TO SHOOT
AND HE STARTED THE INVESTIGATION
   IT'S AGAINST THE LAW
   IT'S AGAINST THE LAW
   WHAT THE MAMA SAW
   WAS AGAINST THE LAW

THE MAMA LOOKED DOWN AND SPIT ON THE GROUND
EVERY TIME MY NAME IS MENTIONED
THE PAPA SAID OY IF I GET THAT BOY
I'M GONNA STICK HIM IN THE HOUSE OF DETENTION
   WELL I'M ON MY WAY
   I DON'T KNOW WHERE I'M GOIN'
   I'M ON MY WAY I'M TAKING MY TIME
   BUT I DON'T KNOW WHERE
   GOODBYE TO ROSIE THE QUEEN OF CORONA
   SEE YOU ME AND JULIO
   DOWN BY THE SCHOOLYARD
   SEE YOU ME AND JULIO
   DOWN BY THE SCHOOLYARD

ME AND JULIO DOWN BY THE SCHOOLYARD

IN A COUPLE OF DAYS THEY COME AND
TAKE ME AWAY
BUT THE PRESS LET THE STORY LEAK
AND WHEN THE RADICAL PRIEST
COME TO GET ME RELEASED
WE WAS ALL ON THE COVER OF NEWSWEEK
  WELL I'M ON MY WAY
   I DON'T KNOW WHERE I'M GOIN'
  I'M ON MY WAY I'M TAKING MY TIME
  BUT I DON'T KNOW WHERE
  GOODBYE TO ROSIE THE QUEEN OF CORONA
  SEE YOU, ME AND JULIO
  DOWN BY THE SCHOOLYARD

79

Me and Julio Down by the Schoolyard

The mama pajama rolled out of bed
And she ran to the police station
When the papa found out, he began to shout
And he started the investigation

It's against the law
It was against the law
What the mama saw
It was against the law

The mama looked down and spit on the ground
Every time my name gets mentioned
The papa said, "Oy, if I get that boy
I'm gonna stick him in the house of detention"

Well, I'm on my way
I don't know where I'm going
I'm on my way
I'm taking my time
But I don't know where
Good-bye to Rosie, the Queen of Corona
See you, me and Julio
Down by the schoolyard
See you, me and Julio
Down by the schoolyard

In a couple of days they come and
Take me away
But the press let the story leak
And when the radical priest
Come to get me released
We was all on the cover of *Newsweek*

80

And I'm on my way
I don't know where I'm going
I'm on my way
I'm taking my time
But I don't know where
Good-bye to Rosie, the Queen of Corona
See you, me and Julio
Down by the schoolyard
See you, me and Julio
Down by the schoolyard

From the album *Paul Simon*

Peace like a river ran through the city
Long past the midnight curfew
We sat starry-eyed
Oh, we were satisfied

And I remember
Misinformation followed us like a plague
Nobody knew from time to time
If the plans were changed
Oh, if the plans were changed

You can beat us with wires
You can beat us with chains
You can run out your rules
But you know you can't outrun the history train
I've seen a glorious day

Four in the morning
I woke up from out of my dreams
Nowhere to go but back to sleep
But I'm reconciled
Oh, oh, oh, I'm gonna be up for a while
Oh, oh, oh, I'm gonna be up for a while
Oh, oh, oh, I'm gonna be up for a while

81

From the album *Paul Simon*

Papa Hobo

It's carbon and monoxide
The ol' Detroit perfume
It hangs on the highways
In the morning
And it lays you down by noon
Oh, Papa Hobo
You can see that I'm dressed like a schoolboy
But I feel like a clown
It's a natural reaction I learned
In this basketball town

Sweep up
I been sweeping up the tips I've made
I been living on Gatorade
Planning my getaway
Detroit, Detroit
Got a hell of a hockey team
Got a left-handed way
Of making a man sign up on that
Automotive dream, oh yeah, oh yeah
Oh, Papa Papa Hobo
Could you slip me a ride?
Well, it's just after breakfast
I'm in the road
And the weatherman lied

82

From the album *Paul Simon*

Paranoia Blues

I got some so-called friends
They'll smile right to my face
But when my back is turned
They'd like to stick it to me
Yes, they would
Oh, no, no
Oh, no, no
There's only one thing I need to know
Whose side are you on?

I fly into JFK
My heart goes boom boom boom
I know that customs man
He's going to take me
To that little room
Oh, no, no
Oh, no, no
There's only one thing I need to know
Whose side are you on?
Whose side are you on?

I got the paranoia blues
From knockin' around in New York City
Where they roll you for a nickel
And they stick you for the extra dime

Any way you choose
You're bound to lose in New York City
Oh, I just got out in the nick of time
Well, I just got out in the nick of time

Once I was down in Chinatown
I was eating some Lin's Chow Fun
I happened to turn around
And when I looked I see
My Chow Fun's gone
Oh, no, no
Oh, no, no
There's only one thing I need to know
Whose side are you on?
Whose side are you on?
Well, there's only one thing I need to know
Whose side, whose side, whose side?

From the album *Paul Simon*

84

Congratulations

Congratulations
Oh, seems like you've done it again
And I ain't had such misery
Since I don't know when
Oh, and I don't know when
Oh, and I don't know when

I notice so many people
Slippin' away
And many more waiting in the lines
In the courtrooms today
Oh, in the courtrooms today

Love is not a game
Love is not a toy
Love's no romance
Love will do you in
And love will wash you out
And needless to say
You won't stand a chance, and you won't stand a chance

85

I'm hungry for learning
Won't you answer me, please?
Can a man and a woman
Live together in peace?
Oh, live together in peace

From the album *Paul Simon*

Paul Simon
There Goes Rhymin' Simon
American Tune
Kodachrome
"KODACHROME"® is a registered trademark for color film.
One Man's Ceiling is Another Man's Floor
Take Me to the Mardi Gras

KODACHROME

WHEN I THINK BACK
ON ALL THE CRAP I LEARNED IN HIGH SCHOOL
IT'S A WONDER
I CAN THINK AT ALL
AND THOUGH MY LACK OF EDUCATION
HASN'T HURT ME NONE
I CAN READ THE WRITING ON THE WALL

KODACHROME
THEY GIVE US THOSE NICE BRIGHT COLORS
THEY GIVE US THE GREENS OF SUMMERS
MAKES YOU THINK ALL THE WORLD'S
A SUNNY DAY
I GOT A NIKON CAMERA
I LOVE TO TAKE A PHOTOGRAPH
SO MAMA DON'T TAKE MY KODACHROME AWAY

IF YOU TOOK ALL THE GIRLS I KNEW
WHEN I WAS SINGLE
AND BROUGHT THEM ALL TOGETHER
FOR ONE NIGHT
I KNOW THEY'D NEVER MATCH
MY SWEET IMAGINATION
EVERYTHING LOOKS WORSE
IN BLACK AND WHITE

KODACHROME   ETC.

Kodachrome

When I think back
On all the crap I learned in high school
It's a wonder
I can think at all
And though my lack of education
Hasn't hurt me none
I can read the writing on the wall

Kodachrome
They give us those nice bright colors
They give us the greens of summers
Makes you think all the world's
A sunny day, oh yeah
I got a Nikon camera
I love to take a photograph
So mama, don't take my Kodachrome away

If you took all the girls I knew
When I was single
And brought them all together
For one night
I know they'd never match
My sweet imagination
Everything looks worse
In black and white

Kodachrome
They give us those nice bright colors
They give us the greens of summers
Makes you think all the world's
A sunny day, oh yeah
I got a Nikon camera
I love to take a photograph
So mama, don't take my Kodachrome away

From the album *There Goes Rhymin' Simon*

88

What can I do?
What can I do?
Much of what you say is true
I know you see through me
But there's no tenderness
Beneath your honesty

Right and wrong
Right and wrong
It never helped us get along
You say you care for me
But there's no tenderness
Beneath your honesty

You and me were such good friends
What's your hurry?
You and me could make amends
I'm not worried
I'm not worried

Honesty
Honesty
It's such a waste of energy
No, you don't have to lie to me
Just give me some tenderness
Beneath your honesty
You don't have to lie to me
Just give me some tenderness

From the album *There Goes Rhymin' Simon*

Come on, take me to the Mardi Gras
Where the people sing and play
Where the dancing is elite
And there's music in the street
Both night and day

Hurry, take me to the Mardi Gras
In the city of my dreams
You can legalize your lows
You can wear your summer clothes
In the New Orleans

And I will lay my burden down
Rest my head upon that shore
And when I wear that starry crown
I won't be wanting anymore

Take your burdens to the Mardi Gras
Let the music wash your soul
You can mingle in the street
You can jingle to the beat
Of Jelly Roll

From the album *There Goes Rhymin' Simon*

Something So Right

You've got the cool water
When the fever runs high
You've got the look of lovelight
In your eyes
And I was in crazy motion
'Til you calmed me down
It took a little time
But you calmed me down

When something goes wrong
I'm the first to admit it
I'm the first to admit it
But the last one to know
When something goes right
Oh, it's likely to lose me
It's apt to confuse me
It's such an unusual sight
Oh, I can't, I can't get used to something so right
Something so right

They got a wall in China
It's a thousand miles long
To keep out the foreigners
They made it strong
And I got a wall around me
That you can't even see
It took a little time
To get next to me

When something goes wrong
I'm the first to admit it
I'm the first to admit it
But the last one to know
When something goes right
Oh, it's likely to lose me
It's apt to confuse me
Because it's such an unusual sight
Oh, I swear, I can't get used to something so right
Something so right

Some people never say the words
"I love you"
It's not their style
To be so bold
Some people never say those words
"I love you"
But like a child, they're longing to be told

When something goes wrong
I'm the first to admit it
I'm the first to admit it
But the last one to know
When something goes right
Oh, it's likely to lose me
It's apt to confuse me
Because it's such an unusual sight
I swear I can't, I can't get used to something so right
Something so right
Something so right

From the album *There Goes Rhymin' Simon*

There's been some hard feelings here
About some words that were said
Been some hard feelings here
And what is more
There's been a bloody purple nose
And some bloody purple clothes
That were messing up the lobby floor
It's just apartment house rules
So all you 'partment house fools
Remember: one man's ceiling
Is another man's floor
One man's ceiling
Is another man's floor

There's been some strange goin's-on
And some folks have come and gone
Like the elevator man don't work no more
I heard a racket in the hall
And I thought I heard a fall
But I never opened up my door
It's just apartment house sense
It's like apartment house rents
Remember: one man's ceiling
Is another man's floor
I tell you, one man's ceiling
Is another man's floor

There's an alley
In the back of my building
Where some people congregate in shame
I was walking with my dogs
And the night was black with smog
When I thought I heard somebody
Call my name
Remember: one man's ceiling
Is another man's floor

From the album *There Goes Rhymin' Simon*

93

AMERICAN TUNE ?

MANY'S THE TIME I'VE BEEN MISTAKEN
AND MANY TIMES CONFUSED
YES, AND OFTEN FELT FORSAKEN
AND CERTAINLY MISUSED
BUT I'M ALL RIGHT, I'M ALL RIGHT
I'M JUST WEARY TO MY BONES
STILL, YOU DON'T EXPECT TO BE
BRIGHT AND BON VIVANT
SO FAR AWAY FROM HOME, SO FAR AWAY FROM HOME

AND I DON'T KNOW A SOUL WHO'S NOT BEEN BATTERED
I DON'T HAVE A FRIEND WHO FEELS AT EASE
I DON'T KNOW A DREAM THAT'S NOT BEEN SHATTERED
OR DRIVEN TO ITS KNEES
BUT IT'S ALL RIGHT, IT'S ALL RIGHT
WE'VE LIVED SO WELL SO LONG
STILL, WHEN I THINK OF THE ROAD
WE'RE TRAVELLING ON
I WONDER WHAT WENT WRONG
I CAN'T HELP IT, I WONDER WHAT WENT WRONG

AND I DREAMED I WAS DYING
AND I DREAMED THAT MY SOUL ROSE UNEXPECTEDLY
AND LOOKING BACK DOWN AT ME
SMILED REASSURINGLY
AND I DREAMED I WAS FLYING
AND HIGH UP ABOVE MY EYES COULD CLEARLY SEE
THE STATUE OF LIBERTY
SAILING AWAY TO SEA
AND I DREAMED I WAS FLYING

Many's the time I've been mistaken
And many times confused
Yes, and I've often felt forsaken
And certainly misused
Oh, but I'm all right, I'm all right
I'm just weary to my bones
Still, you don't expect to be
Bright and bon vivant
So far away from home, so far away from home

I don't know a soul who's not been battered
I don't have a friend who feels at ease
I don't know a dream that's not been shattered
Or driven to its knees
Oh, but it's all right, it's all right
For we've lived so well so long
Still, when I think of the road
We're traveling on
I wonder what's gone wrong
I can't help it, I wonder what's gone wrong

And I dreamed I was dying
I dreamed that my soul rose unexpectedly
And looking back down at me
Smiled reassuringly
And I dreamed I was flying
And high up above, my eyes could clearly see
The Statue of Liberty
Sailing away to sea
And I dreamed I was flying

WE COME ON THE SHIP THEY CALL THE MAYFLOWER
WE COME ON THE SHIP THAT SAILED THE MOON
WE COME IN THE AGE'S MOST UNCERTAIN HOUR
AND SING AN AMERICAN TUNE
BUT IT'S ALL RIGHT, IT'S ALL RIGHT
YOU CAN'T BE FOREVER BLESSED
STILL,
I'VE GOT TO GET SOME REST ?
✓ I'M TRYING TO GET SOME REST

© 1973 Paul Simon

96

Oh, we come on the ship they call the *Mayflower*
We come on the ship that sailed the moon
We come in the age's most uncertain hours
And sing an American tune
Oh, and it's all right
It's all right, it's all right
You can't be forever blessed
Still, tomorrow's going to be another working day
And I'm trying to get some rest
That's all I'm trying to get some rest

From the album *There Goes Rhymin' Simon*

Was a sunny day
Not a cloud was in the sky
Not a negative word was heard
From the peoples passing by
Was a sunny day
All the birdies in the trees
And the radio's singing songs
All the favorite melodies

He was a navy man
Stationed in Newport News
She was a high school queen
With nothing really left to lose
She was a high school queen
With nothing really left to lose

Was a sunny day
Not a cloud was in the sky
Not a negative word was heard
From the peoples passing by
Was a sunny day
All the birdies in the trees
And the radio's singing songs
All the favorite melodies

Her name was Lorelei
She was his only girl
She called him Speedoo
But his Christian name
Was Mr. Earl
She called him Speedoo
But his Christian name
Was Mr. Earl

98

Was a sunny day
Not a cloud was in the sky
Not a negative word was heard
From the peoples passing by

From the album *There Goes Rhymin' Simon*

Learn How to Fall

You got to learn how to fall
Before you learn to fly
And mama, mama, it ain't no lie
Before you learn to fly
Learn how to fall

You got to drift in the breeze
Before you set your sails
Oh, it's an occupation where the wind prevails
Before you set your sails
Drift in the breeze

Oh, and it's the same old story
Ever since the world began
Everybody got the runs for glory
Nobody stop and scrutinize the plan
Nobody stop and scrutinize the plan
Nobody stop and scrutinize the plan

You got to learn how to fall
Before you learn to fly
The tank towns, they tell no lies
Before you learn to fly
Learn how to fall

From the album *There Goes Rhymin' Simon*

St. Judy's Comet

Little sleepy boy
Do you know what time it is?
Well, the hour of your bedtime's
Long been past

And though I know you're fighting it
I can tell when you rub your eyes
You're fading fast
Oo, fading fast

Won't you run come see St. Judy's Comet
Roll across the skies
And leave a spray of diamonds
In its wake
I long to see St. Judy's Comet
Sparkle in your eyes
When you awake
Oh, when you wake, awake

Little boy
Won't you lay your body down?
Little boy
Won't you close your weary eyes?
Ain't nothing flashing but the fireflies

Well, I sang it once
And I sang it twice
I'm going to sing it three times more
Going to stay 'til your resistance
Is overcome
'Cause if I can't sing my boy to sleep
Well, it makes your famous daddy
Look so dumb
Look so dumb

Won't you run come see St. Judy's Comet
Roll across the skies
And leave a spray of diamonds
In its wake
I long to see St. Judy's Comet
Sparkle in your eyes
When you awake
Oh, when you wake, awake

Little boy, little boy
Won't you lay your body down?
Little boy, little boy
Won't you close your weary eyes?
Ain't nothing flashing but the fireflies

Oo, little sleepy boy
Do you know what time it is?
Well, the hour of your bedtime's
Long been past
Though I know you're fighting it
I can tell when you rub your eyes
That you're fading fast
Oo, fading fast

From the album *There Goes Rhymin' Simon*

When I was a little boy
And the Devil would call my name
I'd say, "Now, who do . . .
Who do you think you're fooling?"

I'm a consecrated boy
Singer in a Sunday choir
Oh, my mama loves me, she loves me
She get down on her knees and hug me
Oh, she loves me like a rock
She rock me like the rock of ages
And loves me
She love me, love me, love me, love me

When I was grown to be a man
And the Devil would call my name
I'd say, "Now, who do . . .
Who do you think you're fooling?"

I'm a consummated man
I can snatch a little purity
My mama loves me, she loves me
She get down on her knees and hug me
Oh, she loves me like a rock
She rock me like the rock of ages
And loves me
She love me, love me, love me, love me

LOVES ME LIKE A ROCK

WHEN I WAS A LITTLE BOY
AND THE DEVIL WOULD CALL MY NAME
ID SAY "NOW WHO DO...
WHO DO YOU THINK YOU'RE FOOLING?"
I'M A CONSECRATED BOY
I'M A SINGER IN MY SUNDAY CHOIR
MY MAMA LOVES, SHE LOVES ME
SHE GET DOWN ON HER KNEES AND HUG ME
SHE LOVES ME LIKE A ROCK
SHE ROCKS ME LIKE THE ROCK OF AGES
AND SHE LOVES ME

WHEN I WAS GROWN TO BE A MAN
AND THE DEVIL WOULD CALL MY NAME
I'D SAY "NOW WHO DO...
WHO DO YOU THINK YOU'RE FOOLING?"
I'M A CONSUMATED MAN
I CAN SNATCH A LITTLE PURITY
MY MAMA LOVES ME, SHE LOVES ME
SHE GET DOWN ON HER KNEES AND HUGS ME
SHE LOVES ME LIKE A ROCK
SHE ROCKS ME LIKE THE ROCK OF AGES
AND SHE LOVES ME

IF I WAS THE PRESIDENT
AND THE CONGRESS CALL MY NAME
I'D SAY "WHO DO...
WHO DO YOU THINK YOU'RE FOOLING?"
I GOT THE PRESIDENTIAL SEAL
I'M UP ON THE PRESIDENTIAL PODIUM

If I was president
The minute Congress called my name
I'd say, "Now, who do . . .
Who do you think you're fooling?"

I've got the presidential seal
I'm up on the presidential podium
My mama loves me, she loves me
She get down on her knees and hug me
And she loves me like a rock
She rock me like the rock of ages
And love me
She love me, love me, love me, love me
She love me, love me, love me, love me
She love me, love me, love me, love me

From the album *There Goes Rhymin' Simon*

3   MY MAMA LOVES ME
    SHE LOVES ME
    SHE GET DOWN ON HER KNEES AND HUG ME
    AND SHE LOVES ME LIKE A ROCK
    SHE ROCK ME LIKE THE ROCK OF AGES
    AND SHE LOVES ME
    SHE LOVE ME , LOVE ME, LOVE ME , LOVE ME

        © 1973 Paul Simon

Paul Simon. Still crazy after all these years.

Still Crazy After All These Years

I met my old lover
on the street last night
She seemed so glad to see me
I just smiled
And we talked about some old times
And we drank ourselves some beer
Still crazy after all these years
Still crazy after all these years

I'm not the kind of man
who tends to socialize
I seem to lean on
old familiar ways
And I aint no fool for love songs
That whisper in my ears
Still crazy after all these years
Still crazy after all these years

Four in the morning
crapped out
Yawning
Longing my life away
I'll never worry
Why should I?
It's all gonna fade

Now I sit by my window
and I watch the cars
I fear I'll do some damage
one fine day
But I would not be convicted
by a jury of my peers

Still crazy
Still crazy
Still crazy after all these years.

I met my old lover
On the street last night
She seemed so glad to see me
I just smiled
And we talked about some old times
And we drank ourselves some beers
Still crazy after all these years
Oh, still crazy after all these years

I'm not the kind of man
Who tends to socialize
I seem to lean on old familiar ways
And I ain't no fool for love songs
That whisper in my ears
Still crazy after all these years
Oh, still crazy after all these years

Four in the morning
Crapped out
Yawning
Longing my life away
I'll never worry
Why should I?
It's all gonna fade

Now I sit by my window
And I watch the cars
I fear I'll do some damage
One fine day
But I would not be convicted
By a jury of my peers
Still crazy after all these years
Oh, still crazy
Still crazy
Still crazy after all these years

From the album *Still Crazy After All These Years*

My Little Town

In my little town
I grew up believing
God keeps His eye on us all
And He used to lean upon me
As I pledged allegiance to the wall
Lord, I recall
My little town
Coming home after school
Flying my bike past the gates
Of the factories
My mom doing the laundry
Hanging our shirts
In the dirty breeze

And after it rains
There's a rainbow
And all of the colors are black
It's not that the colors aren't there
It's just imagination they lack
Everything's the same
Back in my little town

Nothing but the dead and dying
Back in my little town
Nothing but the dead and dying
Back in my little town

In my little town
I never meant nothin'
I was just my father's son
Saving my money
Dreaming of glory
Twitching like a finger
On the trigger of a gun
Leaving nothing but the dead and dying
Back in my little town

Nothing but the dead and dying
Back in my little town
Nothing but the dead and dying
Back in my little town

From the album *Still Crazy After All These Years*

110

I Do It for Your Love

We were married on a rainy day
The sky was yellow
And the grass was gray
We signed the papers
And we drove away
I do it for your love

The rooms were musty
And the pipes were old
All that winter we shared a cold
Drank all the orange juice
That we could hold
I do it for your love

Found a rug
In an old junk shop
Brought it home to you
Along the way the colors ran
The orange bled the blue

The sting of reason
The splash of tears
The Northern and the Southern hemispheres
Love emerges and it disappears
I do it for your love
I do it for your love

From the album *Still Crazy After All These Years*

50 WAYS TO LEAVE YOUR LOVER

~~FIFTY WAYS~~

WORDS & MUSIC BY
PAUL SIMON

THE PROBLEM IS ALL INSIDE YOUR HEAD
SHE SAID TO ME
THE ANSWER IS EASY IF YOU
TAKE IT LOGICALLY
I'D LIKE TO HELP you IN YOUR STRUGGLE
TO BE FREE
THERE MUST BE FIFTY WAYS
TO LEAVE YOUR LOVER

SHE SAID IT'S REALLY NOT MY HABIT
TO INTRUDE
FURTHERMORE, I HOPE MY MEANING
WON'T BE LOST OR MISCONSTRUED
BUT I'LL REPEAT MYSELF
AT THE RISK OF BEING CRUDE
THERE MUST BE FIFTY WAYS
TO LEAVE YOUR LOVER
FIFTY WAYS TO LEAVE YOUR LOVER

YOU JUST SLIP OUT THE BACK, JACK
MAKE A NEW PLAN, STAN
YOU DON'T NEED TO BE COY, ROY
JUST ~~AND~~ GET YOURSELF FREE
HOP ON THE BUS, GUS
YOU DON'T NEED TO DISCUSS MUCH
JUST DROP OFF THE KEY, LEE
AND GET YOURSELF FREE

CHORUS

©1975 PAUL SIMON

"The problem is all inside your head"
She said to me
"The answer is easy if you
Take it logically
I'd like to help you in your struggle
To be free
There must be fifty ways
To leave your lover"

She said, "It's really not my habit to intrude
Furthermore, I hope my meaning
Won't be lost or misconstrued
But I'll repeat myself
At the risk of being crude
There must be fifty ways
To leave your lover
Fifty ways to leave your lover"

You just slip out the back, Jack
Make a new plan, Stan
You don't need to be coy, Roy
Just get yourself free
Hop on the bus, Gus
You don't need to discuss much
Just drop off the key, Lee
And get yourself free

Ooh, slip out the back, Jack
Make a new plan, Stan
You don't need to be coy, Roy
Just listen to me
Hop on the bus, Gus
You don't need to discuss much
Just drop off the key, Lee
And get yourself free

She said, "It grieves me so
To see you in such pain
I wish there was something I could do
To make you smile again"
I said, "I appreciate that
And would you please explain
About the fifty ways?"

She said, "Why don't we both
Just sleep on it tonight?
And I believe in the morning
You'll begin to see the light"
And then she kissed me
And I realized she probably was right
There must be fifty ways
To leave your lover
Fifty ways to leave your lover

You just slip out the back, Jack
Make a new plan, Stan
You don't need to be coy, Roy
Just get yourself free
Oh, you hop on the bus, Gus
You don't need to discuss much
Just drop off the key, Lee
And get yourself free

Slip out the back, Jack
Make a new plan, Stan
You don't need to be coy, Roy
You just listen to me
Hop on the bus, Gus
You don't need to discuss much
Just drop off the key, Lee
And get yourself free

From the album *Still Crazy After All These Years*

Night Game

There were two men down
And the score was tied
In the bottom of the eighth
When the pitcher died

And they laid his spikes
On the pitcher's mound
And his uniform was torn
And his number was left on the ground

Then the night turned cold
Colder than the moon
The stars were white as bones
The stadium was old
Older than the screams
Older than the teams

There were three men down
And the season lost
And the tarpaulin was rolled
Upon the winter frost

115

From the album *Still Crazy After All These Years*

The night was black, roads were icy
Snow was fallin', drifts were high
I was weary from my driving
And I stopped to rest for a while
I sat down at a truck stop
I was thinking about my past
I've had a long streak of that bad luck
But I'm praying it's gone at last

Gone at last, gone at last
Gone at last, gone at last
I've had a long streak of that bad luck
But I pray it's gone at last
Oo, oo, oo . . .

I ain't dumb
I've kicked around some
I don't fall too easily
But that girl looked so dejected
She just grabbed my sympathy
Sweet little soul, now, what's your problem?
Tell me why you're so downcast
I've had a long streak of bad luck
But I pray it's gone at last

Gone at last, gone at last
Gone at last, gone at last
I've had a long streak of bad luck
But I pray it's gone at last
Oo, oo, oo . . .

Once in a while, from out of nowhere
When you don't expect it, and you're unprepared
Somebody will come and lift you higher
And your burdens will be shared
Yes, I do believe, if I hadn't met you
I might still be sinking fast
I've had a long streak of bad luck
But I pray it's gone at last

Gone, gone at last, gone at last
Gone at last, gone at last
I've had a long streak of bad luck
But I pray it's gone at last
Oo, oo, oo . . .

From the album *Still Crazy After All These Years*

117

Some Folks' Lives Roll Easy

Some folks' lives roll easy as a breeze
Drifting through a summer night
Heading for a sunny day
But most folks' lives
Oh, they stumble, Lord, they fall
Through no fault of their own
Most folks never catch their stars

And here I am, Lord
I'm knocking at your place of business
I know I ain't got no business here
But you said if I ever got so low
I was busted
You could be trusted

Some folks' lives roll easy
Some folks' lives never roll at all
They just fall
They just fall
Some folks' lives

From the album *Still Crazy After All These Years*

Yesterday, it was my birthday
I hung one more year on the line
I should be depressed
My life's a mess
But I'm having a good time

I've been loving and loving
And loving
I'm exhausted from loving so well
I should go to bed
But a voice in my head
Says, "Ah, what the hell"

Have a good time
Have a good time
Have a good time
Have a good time

Paranoia strikes deep in the heartland
But I think it's all overdone
Exaggerating this, exaggerating that
They don't have no fun

I don't believe what I read in the papers
They're just out to capture my dime
I ain't worrying
And I ain't scurrying
I'm having a good time

Have a good time
IIave a good time
Have a good time
Have a good time

119

Maybe I'm laughing my way to disaster
Maybe my race has been run
Maybe I'm blind
To the fate of mankind
But what can be done?

So God bless the goods we was given
And God bless the U.S. of A.
And God bless our standard of livin'
Let's keep it that way
And we'll all have a good time

Have a good time
Have a good time
Have a good time

From the album *Still Crazy After All These Years*

You're kind
You're so kind
You rescued me when I was blind
And you put me on your pillow
When I was on the wall
You're kind
So kind
So kind

And you're good, you're so good
You introduced me to your neighborhood
Seems like I ain't never had so many friends before
That's because you're good, you're so good

Why you don't treat me like the other humans do
Is just a mystery to me
It gets me agitated when I think that
You're gonna love me now
Indefinitely
So good-bye, good-bye
I'm gonna leave you now
And here's the reason why

121

I like to sleep with the window open
And you keep the window closed
So good-bye
Good-bye
Good-bye

From the album *Still Crazy After All These Years*

Silent Eyes

Silent eyes
Watching
Jerusalem
Make her bed of stones

Silent eyes
No one will comfort her
Jerusalem
Weeps alone

She is sorrow
Sorrow
She burns like a flame
And she calls my name

Silent eyes
Burning
In the desert sun
Halfway to Jerusalem
And we shall all be called as witnesses
Each and every one
To stand before the eyes of God
And speak what was done

122

From the album *Still Crazy After All These Years*

He was a mean individual
He had a heart like a bone
He was a naturally crazy man
And better off left alone
Well, he stopped one night
At a traffic light
And when that light turned green
He was a mean individual
Stranded in a limousine

Hey hey hey hey
All the children in the street
They come running out their front door
Running out their back door
Flying on their feet
They said, "Mama, oh! Papa, oh!
See what I have seen
There's a mean individual stranded in a limousine"

Then everybody came running
Ev'rybody said, "Lord! Lord!"
Ev'rybody was gunning
They're gonna divvy up the reward
And then a wah wah wah wah wah wah wah
There's a siren, a flashing light
But the mean individual
He vanished in the black of night

123

Hey hey hey hey
They wondered where to begin
'Cause he left that neighborhood
Just like a rattlesnake sheds its skin
Well they searched the roofs
And they checked out the groups
And they photographed the scene
For the mean individual
Stranded in a limousine

Then everybody came running
Ev'rybody said, "Lord! Lord!"
Ev'rybody was gunning
They're gonna divvy up the reward
And then a wah wah wah wah wah wah wah
There's a siren, a flashing light
But the mean individual
He vanished in the black of night

Slip Slidin' Away

Slip slidin' away
Slip slidin' away
You know the nearer your destination
The more you're slip slidin' away

I know a man
He came from my hometown
He wore his passion for his woman
Like a thorny crown
He said, "Delores, I live in fear
My love for you's so overpowering
I'm afraid that I will disappear"

Slip slidin' away
Slip slidin' away
You know the nearer your destination
The more you're slip slidin' away

And I know a woman
Became a wife
These are the very words she uses to describe her life
She said, "A good day
Ain't got no rain"
She said, "A bad day's when I lie in bed
And think of things that might have been"

125

Slip slidin' away
Slip slidin' away
You know the nearer your destination
The more you're slip slidin' away

And I know a father
Who had a son
He longed to tell him all the reasons
For the things he'd done
He came a long way
Just to explain
He kissed his boy as he lay sleeping
Then he turned around and headed home again

Slip slidin' away
Slip slidin' away
You know the nearer your destination
The more you're slip slidin' away

God only knows
God makes his plan
The information's unavailable
To the mortal man
We're working our jobs
Collect our pay
Believe we're gliding down the highway
When in fact we're slip slidin' away

Slip slidin' away
Slip slidin' away
You know the nearer your destination
The more you're slip slidin' away

SLIP SLIDING AWAY

Slip Sliding Away
"   "   "

You know the nearer your destination
The more you're slip sliding away

I know a man
He came from my home town
He wore this passion for his woman
like a thorny crown
He said Delores
I live in fear
My love ours's so overpowering
I'm afraid that I will disappear

CHORUS

I know a woman
became a wife
These are the very words she uses
To describe her life
She said a good day
ain't got no rain
She said a bad day's when I lie in bed
And think of things that might have been
CHORUS

1978-1983

One-Trick Pony
Late in the Evening
That's Why God Made the Movies
One-Trick Pony
How the Heart Approaches
    What It Yearns
Oh, Marion
Ace in the Hole
Nobody
Jonah
God Bless the Absentee
Long, Long Day
Additional lyrics:
Soft Parachutes
Slow Man
Spiral Highway

Hearts and Bones
Allergies
Hearts and Bones
When Numbers Get Serious
Think Too Much (b)
Song About the Moon
Think Too Much (a)
Train in the Distance
René and Georgette Magritte
    with Their Dog After the War
Cars Are Cars
The Late Great Johnny Ace
Additional lyrics:
Shelter of Your Arms
Citizen of the Planet

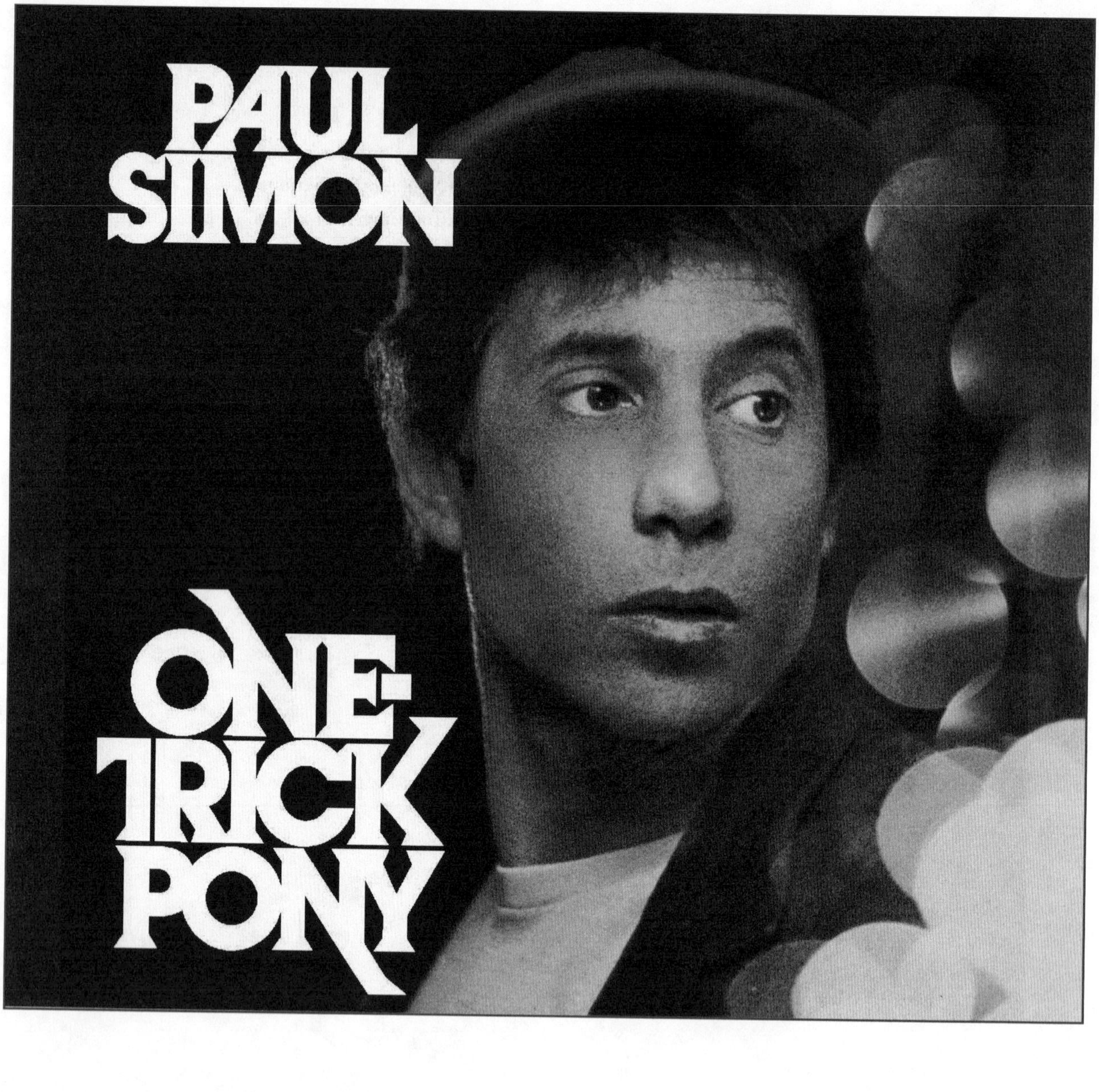
PAUL
SIMON
ONE-
TRICK
PONY

Late in the Evening

First thing I remember
I was lying in my bed
Couldn't've been no more
Than one or two
I remember there's a radio
Comin' from the room next door
And my mother laughed
The way some ladies do
When it's late in the evening
And the music's seeping through

The next thing I remember
I am walking down the street
I'm feeling all right
I'm with my boys
I'm with my troops, yeah
And down along the avenue
Some guys were shootin' pool
And I heard the sound of a cappella groups, yeah
Singing late in the evening
And all the girls out on the stoops, yeah

Then I learned to play some lead guitar
I was underage in this funky bar
And I stepped outside to smoke myself a "J"
And when I come back to the room
Everybody just seemed to move
And I turned my amp up loud and I began to play
And it was late in the evening
And I blew that room away

First thing I remember
When you came into my life
I said, "I'm gonna get that girl
No matter what I do"
Well, I guess I'd been in love before
And once or twice I'd been on the floor
But I never loved no one
The way that I loved you
And it was late in the evening
And all the music seeping through

From the album *One-Trick Pony*

132

That's Why God Made the Movies

When I was born my mother died
She said, "Bye-bye, baby, bye-bye"
I said, "Where you goin'? I'm just born"
She said, "I'll only be gone for a while"
My mother loved to leave in style
That's why God made the movies

Well, I laid around in my swaddling clothes
Until the doctor came and turned out the light
Then I packed my bag
And my name tag
I stole away into the night
Hoping things would work out right
That's why God made the movies

Say you will, say you will
Say you'll take me to your lovin' breast
Say you'll nourish me
With your tenderness
The way the ladies sometimes do
Say you won't, say you won't
Say you won't leave me for no other man
Say you'll love me just the way I am
Say you will, baby, now
Say you will, just say you will
Say you will

When I was born my mother died
She said, "Bye-bye, baby, bye-bye"
And since that day
I've made my way
The notorious boy of the wild
Adopted by the wolves when he was a child

That's why God
That's why God
That's why God made the movies

From the album *One-Trick Pony*

134

One-Trick Pony

He's a one-trick pony
One trick is all that horse can do
He does one trick only
It's the principal source of his revenue
And when he steps into the spotlight
You can feel the heat of his heart
Come rising through

See how he dances
See how he loops from side to side
See how he prances
The way his hooves just seem to glide
He's just a one-trick pony, that's all he is
But he turns that trick with pride

He makes it look so easy
It looks so clean
He moves like God's
Immaculate machine
He makes me think about
All of these extra moves I make
And all this herky-jerky motion
And the bag of tricks it takes
To get me through my working day
One-trick pony

He's a one-trick pony
He either fails or he succeeds
He gives his testimony
Then he relaxes in the weeds
He's got one trick to last a lifetime
But that's all a pony needs, that's all he needs

He looks so easy
It looks so clean
He moves like God's
Immaculate machine
He makes me think about
All of these extra moves I make
And all this herky-jerky motion
And the bag of tricks it takes
To get me through my working day
One-trick pony
One-trick pony

One-trick pony, one-trick pony
One-trick pony—take me for a ride
One-trick pony

From the album *One-Trick Pony*

In the blue light
Of the Belvedere Motel
Wondering as the television burns
How the heart approaches what it yearns

In a fever
I distinctly hear your voice
Emerging from a dream, the dream returns
How the heart approaches what it yearns

After the rain on the interstate
Headlights slide past the moon
A bone-weary traveler waits
By the side of the road
Where's he going?

I dream we are lying on the top of a hill
And headlights slide past the moon
I roll in your arms
And your voice is the heat of the night
I'm on fire

137

In a phone booth
In some local bar and grill
Rehearsing what I'll say, my coin returns
How the heart approaches what it yearns
How the heart approaches what it yearns

From the album *One-Trick Pony*

The boy's got brains
He just don't use 'em, that's all
The boy's got brains
He just refuse to use 'em, and that's all
He says, "The more I get to thinking
The less I tend to laugh"
The boy's got brains
He just abstains

The boy's got a heart
But it beats on his opposite side
It's a strange phenomenon
The laws of nature defied
He said, "It's a chance I had to take
So I shifted my heart for its safety's sake"
The boy's got a heart, but it beats on
His opposite

Oh, Marion
I think I'm in trouble here
I should've believed you
When I heard you saying it
The only time
That love is an easy game
Is when two other people
Are playing it

The boy's got a voice
But the voice is his natural disguise
Yes, the boy's got a voice
But his words don't connect to his eyes
He says, "Ah, but when I sing
I can hear the truth auditioning"
The boy's got a voice
But the voice is his natural

Oh, Marion
I think I'm in trouble here
I should've believed you
When I heard you saying it
The only time
That love is an easy game
Is when two other people
Are playing it

From the album *One-Trick Pony*

139

Some people say Jesus, that's the ace in the hole
But I never met the man so I don't really know
Maybe some Christmas, if I'm sick and alone
He will look up my number
Call me on the phone, and say
"Hey, boy, where you been so long?
Don't you know me?
I'm your ace in the hole"

Two hundred dollars, that's my ace in the hole
When I'm down, dirty and desperate
That's my emergency bankroll
I got two hundred dollars, that's the price on the street
If you wanna get some quality
That's the price you got to meet
And the man says
"Hey, Junior, where you been so long?
Don't you know me?
I'm your ace in the hole"
Talkin' about ace in the hole

Once I was crazy and my ace in the hole
Was that I knew that I was crazy
So I never lost my self-control
I just walk in the middle of the road and
I sleep in the middle of the bed
I stop in the middle of a sentence
And the voice in the middle of my head said
"Hey, Junior, where you been so long?
Don't you know me?
I'm your ace in the hole"

Ace in the hole
Lean on me
Don't you know me?
I'm your guarantee

Riding on this rolling bus
Beneath a stony sky
With a slow moon rising
And the smokestacks drifting by
In the hour when the heart is weakest
And memory is strong
When time has stopped
And the bus just rolls along
Roll on, roll on
Roll on, roll on
Roll on, roll on

Some people say music, that's their ace in the hole
Just your ordinary rhythm and blues
Your basic rock and roll
You can sit on the top of the beat
You can lean on the side of the beat
You can hang from the bottom of the beat
But you got to admit that the music is sweet

141

Where you been so long
Don't you know me?
I'm your ace in the hole, oh yeah

Ace in the hole
Lean on me
Don't you know me?
I'm your guarantee

From the album *One-Trick Pony*

Nobody

Who knows my secret broken bone?
Who feels my flesh when I am gone?
Who was a witness to the dream?
Who kissed my eyes and saw the scream
Lying there?
Nobody

Who is my reason to begin?
Who plows the earth, who breaks the skin?
Who took my two hands and made them four?
Who is my heart, who is my door?
Nobody

Nobody but you, girl
Nobody but you
Nobody in this whole wide world
Nobody

Who makes the bed that can't be made?
Who is my mirror, who's my blade?
When I am rising like a flood
Who feels the pounding in my blood?
Nobody

Nobody but you
Nobody but you, girl
Nobody in this whole wide world
Nobody, girl
Nobody

Nobody but you
Nobody but you
Nobody in this whole wide world
Nobody, nobody
Nobody

From the album *One-Trick Pony*

Jonah

Half an hour, change your strings and tune up
Sizing the room up
Checking the bar
Local girls, unspoken conversation
Misinformation
Plays guitar

They say Jonah, he was swallowed by a whale
But I say there's no truth to that tale
I know Jonah
He was swallowed by a song

No one gives their dreams away too lightly
They hold them tightly
Warm against cold
One more year of traveling 'round this circuit
Then you can work it into gold

They say Jonah, he was swallowed by a whale
But I say there's no truth to that tale
I know Jonah
He was swallowed by a song

Here's to all the boys who came along
Carrying soft guitars in cardboard cases
All night long
And do you wonder where those boys have gone?
Do you wonder where those boys have gone?

From the album *One-Trick Pony*

God Bless the Absentee

Lord, I am a working man
And music is my trade
I'm traveling with this five-piece band
I play the ace of spades
I have a wife and family, but they don't see much of me
God bless the absentee

Lord, I am a surgeon
And music is my knife
It cuts away my sorrow
And purifies my life
But if I could release my heart
From veins and arteries
I'd say, God bless the absentee

I miss my woman so
I miss my bed
I miss those soft places
I used to lay my head
My son don't need me yet
His bones are soft
He flies a silver airplane
He wears a golden cross
God bless the absentee

Lord, this country's changed so fast
The future is the present
The present's in the past
The highways are in litigation
The airports disagree
God bless the absentee
God bless the absentee

From the album *One-Trick Pony*

Long, Long Day (Duet)

It's been a long, long day
I got some run-down shoes
Ain't got no place to stay
But any old place will be okay
It's been a long, long day

Good night
Good night
Oh, my love

I've sure been on this road
Done nearly fourteen years
Can't say my name's well known
You don't see my face in *Rolling Stone*
But I've sure been on this road

Good night
Good night
My love

When I saw him standing there
I said, "Hey, there's a guy who needs a laugh" (Slow motion)
That's what I said to myself (Half a dollar bill)

What the hell, we're both alone
And I'm just standing here
Jukebox in the corner
Shooting to kill
And it's been a . . .

It's been a long, long day
I sure could use a friend
Don't know what else to say
I hate to abuse an old cliché
But it's been a long, long day
It's been a long, long day

From the album *One-Trick Pony*

Soft Parachutes

Soft parachutes, Fourth of July
And villages burning
Returning the bodies, all laid in a line
Like soft parachutes

Last year, I was a senior
In Emerson High School
I had me a girlfriend
We used to get high
And now I am flying
Down some Vietnam highway
Don't ask me the reason
God only knows why

Soft parachutes, Fourth of July
And villages burning
Returning the bodies, all laid in a line
Soft parachutes

146

Slow Man

Slow man
Movin' down the road
He's movin' with a leisurely gait
Slow man
Doesn't overload
He just travels with his bodily weight

"It doesn't matter to me
It doesn't matter at all"
Said the slow man
"It doesn't matter to me
I got a feelin'
Yes, indeed
That's all I need
That's all, that's all"

Slow man
Sittin' in the sun
Doesn't worry 'bout the chance of rain
Slow man
With the suntan
Got no reason to complain

"It doesn't matter to me
It doesn't matter at all"
Said the slow man
"It doesn't matter to me
I got a feelin'
Yes, indeed
That's all I need
That's all, that's all"

But I'm workin' at a furious pace
From the mornin' 'til the end of the day
Me, oh Lord, look at these lines upon my face
I got to figure out a better way

Slow man
Purchases a comb
Though he doesn't have a wisp of hair
Slow man
Doesn't own a home
But he's comfortable everywhere

But slow man, sittin' in the sun
Doesn't worry 'bout the chance of rain
Slow man with the suntan
Got no reason to complain

"You got to get the slow in your life"
Said the slow man
"You got to get the slow in your life
Got to get the slow in your life"
Said the slow man
You got to

Spiral Highway (Fragment)

Every bar and grill
Every greasy spoon
Anywhere a quarter buys a tune
Ride that spiral highway one more round

Every local call
From every pink motel
Any time the strain begins to tell
Ride that spiral highway one more round

After the rain on the interstate
Headlights slide past the moon
A bone-weary traveler waits by the side of the road
Where's he going?

Then I think it's strange
The way the body turns
How the heart approaches what it yearns
Ride that spiral highway one more round
Ride that spiral highway one more round

149

Allergies

Maladies
Melodies
Allergies to dust and grain
Maladies
Remedies
Still these allergies remain

My hands can't touch a guitar string
My fingers just burn and ache
My head intercedes with my bodily needs
And my body won't give it a break
My heart can stand a disaster
My heart can take a disgrace
But my heart is allergic
To the women I love
And it's changing the shape of my face

Allergies
Allergies
Something's living on my skin
Doctor, please
Doctor, please
Open up, it's me again

I go to a famous physician
I sleep in the local hotel
From what I can see of the people like me
We get better
But we never get well
So I ask myself this question
It's a question I often repeat
Where do allergies go
When it's after a show
And they want to get something to eat?

Allergies
Allergies
Something's living on my skin
Doctor, please
Doctor, please
Open up, it's me again
Maladies
Melodies
Allergies to dust and grain
Maladies
Remedies
Still these allergies remain
(I can't breathe)

Allergies
Allergies
Something's living on my skin
Doctor, please
Doctor, please
Open up, it's me again

Allergies
Allergies
Allergies

From the album *Hearts and Bones*

One and one-half wandering Jews
Free to wander wherever they choose
Are traveling together
In the Sangre de Cristo
The Blood of Christ Mountains
Of New Mexico
On the last leg of the journey
They started a long time ago
The arc of a love affair
Rainbows in the high desert air
Mountain passes slipping into stones
Hearts and bones
Hearts and bones
Hearts and bones

Thinking back to the season before
Looking back through the cracks in the door
Two people were married
The act was outrageous
The bride was contagious
She burned like a bride
These events may have had some effect
On the man with the girl by his side
The arc of a love affair
His hands rolling down her hair
Love like lightning, shaking till it moans
Hearts and bones
Hearts and bones
Hearts and bones

153

And whoa, whoa, whoa
She said, "Why?
Why don't we drive through the night?
We'll wake up down in
Mexico"
Oh, I
I don't know nothin' about, nothin' about no
Mexico
"And tell me why
Why won't you love me
For who I am
Where I am?"

He said, "'Cause that's not the way the world is, baby
This is how I love you, baby
This is how I love you, baby"

One and one-half wandering Jews
Returned to their natural coasts
To resume old acquaintances
And step out occasionally
And speculate who had been damaged the most
Easy time will determine if these consolations
Will be their reward
The arc of a love affair
Waiting to be restored
You take two bodies and you twirl them into one
Their hearts and their bones
And they won't come undone
Hearts and bones
Hearts and bones
Hearts and bones

From the album *Hearts and Bones*

I have a number in my head
Though I don't know why it's there
When numbers get serious
You see their shape everywhere
Dividing and multiplying
Exchanging with ease
When times are mysterious
Serious numbers are eager to please

Take my address
Take my phone
Call me if you can
Here's my address
Here's my phone
Now, please don't give it to some madman
Hey hey, whoa whoa
It's a complicated life
Numbers swirling, thick and curious
You can cut them with a knife
You can cut them with a knife

Two times two is twenty-two
Four times four is forty-four
When numbers get serious
They leave a mark on your door
Urgent! Urgent!
A telephone ringing in the hallways
When times are mysterious
Serious numbers will speak to us always

That is why a man with numbers
Can put your mind at ease
We've got numbers by the trillions
Here and overseas
Hey hey, whoa whoa
Look at that stink about Japan
All those numbers waiting patiently
Now, don't you understand?
Don't you understand?

So wrap me
Wrap me
Wrap me do
In the shelter of your arms
I am ever your volunteer
I won't do you any harm
I will love you innumerably
You can count on my word
When times are mysterious
Serious numbers will always be heard
When times are mysterious
Serious numbers will always be heard

156

And after all is said and done
And the numbers all come home
The four rolls into three
Three turns into two
And the two becomes a
One

From the album *Hearts and Bones*

Think Too Much (b)

The smartest people in the world
Had gathered in Los Angeles
To analyze our love affair
And finally unscramble us
And they sat among our photographs
Examined every one
And in the end, we compromised
And met the morning sun

Maybe I think too much
Maybe I think too much
Oh, maybe I think too much
Maybe I think too much

They say the left side of the brain
Dominates the right
And the right side has to labor through
The long and speechless night
And in the night
My father came to me
And held me to his chest
He said, "There's not much more that you can do
Go home and get some rest"

And I said, yeah
Maybe I think too much
Maybe I think too much
Oh, maybe I think too much
Maybe I think too much

From the album *Hearts and Bones*

If you want to write a song about the moon
Walk along the craters in the afternoon
When the shadows are deep and the light is alien
And gravity leaps like a knife off the pavement
And you want to write a song about the moon
You want to write a spiritual tune
Na na na na na na
Yeah yeah yeah
Presto, song about the moon

If you want to write a song about the heart
Think about the moon before you start
Because the heart will howl like a dog in the moonlight
And the heart can explode like a pistol on a June night
So if you want to write a song about the heart
And its ever longing for a counterpart
Na na na na na na
Yeah yeah yeah
Write a song about the moon

The laughing boy, he laughed so hard
He fell down from his place
The laughing girl, she laughed so hard
Tears rolled down her face
Wo wo

Hey, songwriter
If you want to write a song about a face
Think about a photograph
That you really can't remember but you can't erase
Wash your hands and dreams in lightning
Cut off your hair and whatever is frightening
If you want to write a song about a face
If you want to write a song about the human race
Na na na na na na
Yeah yeah yeah
Write a song about the moon

Oh oh oh oh oh

If you want to write a song about the moon
You want to write a spiritual tune
Na na na na na na
Yeah yeah yeah
Then do it!
Write a song about the moon

From the album *Hearts and Bones*

They say that the left side of the brain
Controls the right
They say that the right side
Has to work hard all night
Maybe I think too much for my own good
Some people say so
Other people say, "No, no
The fact is
You don't think as much as you could"

I had a childhood that was mercifully brief
I grew up in a state of disbelief
I started to think too much
When I was twelve going on thirteen
Me and the girls from St. Augustine
Up in the mezzanine
Thinking about God

Maybe I think too much
Maybe I think too much
Maybe I think too much
Maybe I think too much

Have you ever experienced a period of grace
When your brain just takes a seat behind your face?
And the world begins the Elephant Dance
Everything's funny
Everyone's sunny
You take out your money
And walk down the road
That leads me to the girl I love
The girl I'm always thinking of
But maybe I think too much
And I ought to just hold her
Stop trying to mold her
Maybe blindfold her
And take her away

Maybe I think too much
Maybe I think too much
Maybe I think too much
Maybe I think too much

From the album *Hearts and Bones*

She was beautiful as Southern skies the night he met her
She was married to someone
He was doggedly determined that he would get her
He was old, he was young

From time to time he'd tip his heart
But each time she withdrew
Everybody loves the sound of a train in the distance
Everybody thinks it's true
Everybody loves the sound of a train in the distance
Everybody thinks it's true

Well, eventually the boy and the girl get married
Sure enough, they have a son
And though they both were occupied with the child she carried
Disagreements had begun

And in a while they just fell apart
It wasn't hard to do
Everybody loves the sound of a train in the distance
Everybody thinks it's true
Everybody loves the sound of a train in the distance
Everybody thinks it's true

Two disappointed believers
Two people playing the game
Negotiations and love songs
Are often mistaken for one and the same

Now the man and the woman, they remain in contact
Let us say it's for the child
With disagreements about the meaning of a marriage contract
Conversations hard and wild

But from time to time, he just makes her laugh
She cooks a meal or two
Everybody loves the sound of a train in the distance
Everybody thinks it's true
Everybody loves the sound of a train in the distance
Everybody thinks it's true

What is the point of this story?
What information pertains?
The thought that life could be better
Is woven indelibly
Into our hearts
And our brains

From the album *Hearts and Bones*

René and Georgette Magritte with Their Dog After the War

René and Georgette Magritte
With their dog after the war
Returned to their hotel suite
And they unlocked the door

Easily losing their evening clothes
They dance by the light of the moon
To the Penguins
The Moonglows
The Orioles
And the Five Satins
The deep, forbidden music
They'd been longing for
René and Georgette Magritte
With their dog after the war

René and Georgette Magritte
With their dog after the war
Were strolling down Christopher Street
When they stopped in a men's store
With all of the mannequins
Dressed in style
That brought tears to their
Immigrant eyes

Just like the Penguins
The Moonglows
The Orioles
And the Five Satins
The easy stream of laughter
Flowing through the air
René and Georgette Magritte
With their dog *après la guerre*

Side by side
They fell asleep
Decades gliding by like Indians
Time is cheap
When they wake up, they will find
All their personal belongings
Have intertwined

René and Georgette Magritte
With their dog after the war
Were dining with the power élite
And they looked in their bedroom drawer
And what do you think
They have hidden away
In the cabinet cold of their hearts?

The Penguins
The Moonglows
The Orioles
And the Five Satins
For now and ever after
As it was before
René and Georgette Magritte
With their dog
After the war

From the album *Hearts and Bones*

165

Cars are cars
All over the world
Cars are cars
All over the world
Similarly made
Similarly sold
In a motorcade
Abandoned when they're old
Cars are cars
All over the world

Cars are cars
All over the world
Cars are cars
All over the world
Engine in the front
Jack in the back
Wheels take the brunt
Pinion and a rack

166

Cars are cars
All over the world
Cars are cars
All over the world

But people are strangers
They change with the curve
From time zone to time zone
As we can observe
They shut down their borders
And think they're immune
They stand on their differences
And shoot at the moon

But cars are cars
All over the world
Cars are cars
All over the world
Drive 'em on the left
Drive 'em on the right
Susceptible to theft
In the middle of the night

Cars are cars
All over the world
Cars are cars
All over the world
Cars are cars
All over the world

I once had a car
That was more like a home
I lived in it, loved in it
Polished its chrome
If some of my homes
Had been more like my car
I probably wouldn't have
Traveled this far

Cars are cars
All over the world
Cars are cars
All over the world
Cars are cars
All over the world

167

From the album *Hearts and Bones*

I was reading a magazine
And thinking of a rock and roll song
The year was 1954
And I hadn't been playing that long
When a man came on the radio
And this is what he said
He said, "I hate to break it
To his fans
But Johnny Ace is dead"

Well, I really wasn't
Such a Johnny Ace fan
But I felt bad all the same
So I sent away for his photograph
And I waited till it came
It came all the way from Texas
With a sad and simple face
And they signed it on the bottom
"From the Late Great Johnny Ace"

168

It was the year of the Beatles
It was the year of the Stones
It was 1964
I was living in London
With the girl from the summer before
It was the year of the Beatles
It was the year of the Stones
A year after JFK
We were staying up all night
And giving the days away
And the music was flowing
Amazing
And blowing my way

On a cold December evening
I was walking through the Christmas tide
When a stranger came up and asked me
If I'd heard John Lennon had died
And the two of us
Went to this bar
And we stayed to close the place
And every song we played
Was for the Late Great Johnny Ace

From the album *Hearts and Bones*

Shelter of Your Arms

Wrap me
Wrap me
Wrap me do
In the shelter of your arms
I'm an extraordinary individual
I won't do you no harm
And I won't tell you no lies
If you don't want me to
But if you want me to, I'll lie
In the shelter of your arms
In the palm of your embrace
I could deny the obvious
I could rest my case
And I don't rest my case for no one
If I'm not in the mood to
When I'm in the mood, I try
Take a long look at these laugh lines
They go halfway around the block
In the shelter of your arms, I stop the clock
I stop the clock
I stop the clock

I lived a year once in a hotel
'Cause I failed to read a sign
For a long time I was miserable
Then I felt just fine
And now I feel so fine so often
I'm like a textbook case
Just a textbook of fine
In the shelter of your arms

Wrap me
Wrap me
Wrap me do
In the shelter of your arms
I'm an extraordinary individual
And I won't do you no harm
I won't tell you no lies
Unless you want me to
But if you want me to, I'll lie
Lie in the shelter of your arms
In the palm of your embrace

I am a citizen of the planet
I was born here
I'm going to die here
Come what may
I am entitled by my birth
To the treasures of the earth
No one must be denied these
No one must be denied
Easy dreams
At the end of a chain-smokin' day
Easy dreams at the end of the day

Who am I to believe
That the future we perceive
Lies in danger, and the dangers increase?
Who are we to demand
That the leaders of the land
Hear the voices of reason and peace?

We are the citizens of the planet
We were born here
We're going to die here
Come what may
We are entitled by our birth
To the treasures of the earth
No one must be denied these
No one must be denied
Easy dreams at the end of a chain-smokin' day
Easy dreams at the end of the day

Who am I to deny
What my eyes can clearly see?
And raise a child with a flame in his heart
Who are we to believe
That these dreams are just naïve
When we've all disagreed from the start?

We are the citizens of the planet
We were born here
We're gong to die here
Come what may
We are entitled by our birth
To the treasures of the earth
No one must be denied these
No one must be denied
Easy dreams at the end of a chain-smokin' day
Easy dreams at the end of the day

1984-1990

Graceland

The Boy in the Bubble

Graceland

I Know What I Know

Gumboots

Diamonds on the Soles of Her
  Shoes

You Can Call Me Al

Under African Skies

Homeless

Crazy Love, Vol. II

That Was Your Mother

All Around the World or The Myth
  of Fingerprints

Additional lyrics:

Changing Opinion

The Rhythm of the Saints

The Obvious Child

Can't Run But

The Coast

Proof

Further to Fly

She Moves On

Born at the Right Time

The Cool, Cool River

Spirit Voices

The Rhythm of the Saints

Additional lyrics:

Thelma

Ten Years

PAUL · SIMON
GRACELAND

Boy In The Bubble

Hey Tom
This is the dream
That urged me awake
of moonlight flapping — sliding
on a midnight lake

The newborn wailing in oxygen earthquake

The rhythm of resistance
heart pumping into daybreak

We come
spun out of blackness
colored by rain
All of the colors of the atmosphere

Everything will end now
Everything can start

Every generation throws a
hero up the chart

Medicine is magic
magical is art

Boy in a bubble
Baby with a baboon heart

It was a slow day
And the sun was beating
On the soldiers by the side of the road
There was a bright light
A shattering of shopwindows
The bomb in the baby carriage
Was wired to the radio

These are the days of miracle and wonder
This is the long-distance call
The way the camera follows us in slo-mo
The way we look to us all
The way we look to a distant constellation
That's dying in a corner of the sky
These are the days of miracle and wonder
And don't cry, baby, don't cry
Don't cry

It was a dry wind
And it swept across the desert
And it curled into the circle of birth
And the dead sand was
Falling on the children
The mothers and the fathers
And the automatic earth

These are the days of miracle and wonder
This is the long-distance call
The way the camera follows us in slo-mo
The way we look to us all
The way we look to a distant constellation
That's dying in the corner of the sky
These are the days of miracle and wonder
And don't cry, baby, don't cry
Don't cry

It's a turnaround jump shot
It's everybody jump-start
It's every generation throws a hero up the pop charts
Medicine is magical and magical is art
Think of the Boy in the Bubble
And the baby with the baboon heart

And I believe
These are the days of lasers in the jungle
Lasers in the jungle somewhere
Staccato signals of constant information
A loose affiliation of millionaires
And billionaires, and baby

These are the days of miracle and wonder
This is the long-distance call
The way the camera follows us in slo-mo
The way we look to us all, oh yeah
The way we look to a distant constellation
That's dying in a corner of the sky
These are the days of miracle and wonder
And don't cry, baby, don't cry
Don't cry, don't cry

179

From the album *Graceland*

Sync.
double guitar
line in verses
Trumpets & sax in
sync or acoustic
in chorus

Graceland

3/31/85

Chorus

We're going to Graceland
Graceland
In Memphis Tennessee

I'm going to Graceland

For no logical reason }
                    no explanation
But something But the
feeling that
Something deep inside of me

Is going to Graceland

My travelling companion
I only in his turn
In fact he my boy in
from his first marriage
He looks
They sit in the depot
Back at
He sits on the motel

Graceland

The Mississippi Delta
Was shining like a National guitar
I am following the river
Down the highway
Through the cradle of the Civil War

I'm going to Graceland
Graceland
In Memphis, Tennessee
I'm going to Graceland
Poor boys and pilgrims with families
And we are going to Graceland
My traveling companion is nine years old
He is the child of my first marriage
But I've reason to believe
We both will be received
In Graceland

She comes back to tell me she's gone
As if I didn't know that
As if I didn't know my own bed
As if I'd never noticed
The way she brushed her hair from her forehead
And she said, "Losing love
Is like a window in your heart
Everybody sees you're blown apart
Everybody feels the wind blow"

I'm going to Graceland
Memphis, Tennessee
I'm going to Graceland
Poor boys and pilgrims with families
And we are going to Graceland
And my traveling companions
Are ghosts and empty sockets
I'm looking at ghosts and empties
But I've reason to believe
We all will be received
In Graceland

There is a girl in New York City
Who calls herself the human trampoline
And sometimes when I'm falling, flying
Or tumbling in turmoil I say
Whoa, so this is what she means
She means we're bouncing into Graceland
And I see losing love
Is like a window in your heart
Everybody sees you're blown apart
Everybody feels the wind blow

In Graceland, in Graceland
I'm going to Graceland
For reasons I cannot explain
There's some part of me wants to see Graceland
And I may be obliged to defend
Every love, every ending
Or maybe there's no obligations now
Maybe I've a reason to believe
We all will be received
In Graceland

Whoa, in Graceland, in Graceland
In Graceland
I'm going to Graceland

From the album *Graceland*

She looked me over
And I guess she thought
I was all right
All right in a sort of a limited way
For an off-night
She said, "Don't I know you
From the cinematographer's party?"
I said, "Who am I
To blow against the wind?"

I know what I know
I'll sing what I said
We come and we go
That's a thing that I keep
In the back of my head

I know what I know
I'll sing what I said
We come and we go
That's a thing that I keep
In the back of my head

She said, "There's something about you
That really reminds me of money"
She was the kind of a girl
Who could say things that
Weren't that funny
I said, "What does that mean
I really remind you of money?"
She said, "Who am I
To blow against the wind?"

I know what I know
I'll sing what I said
We come and we go
That's a thing that I keep
In the back of my head

I know what I know
I'll sing what I said
We come and we go
That's a thing that I keep
In the back of my head

She moved so easily
All I could think of was sunlight
I said, "Aren't you the woman
Who was recently given a Fulbright?"
She said, "Don't I know you
From the cinematographer's party?"
I said, "Who am I
To blow against the wind?"

I know what I know
I'll sing what I said
We come and we go
That's a thing that I keep
In the back of my head

I know what I know
I'll sing what I said
We come and we go
That's a thing that I keep
In the back of my head

I know what I know
I know what I know

From the album *Graceland*

Gumboots

I was having this discussion
In a taxi heading downtown
Rearranging my position
On this friend of mine who had
A little bit of a breakdown
I said, "Hey, you know, breakdowns come
And breakdowns go
So what are you going to do about it?
That's what I'd like to know"

You don't feel you could love me
But I feel you could

It was in the early morning hours
When I fell into a phone call
Believing I had supernatural powers
I slammed into a brick wall
I said, "Hey, is this my problem?
Is this my fault?
If that's the way it's gonna be
I'm gonna call the whole thing to a halt"

You don't feel you could love me
But I feel you could
You don't feel you could love me
But I feel you could

I was walking down the street
When I thought I heard this voice say
"Say, ain't we walking down the same street together
On the very same day?"
I said, "Hey, Señorita, that's astute"
I said, "Why don't we get together
And call ourselves an institute?"

You don't feel you could love me
But I feel you could
You don't feel you could love me
But I feel you could

I was having this discussion
In a taxi heading downtown . . .

From the album *Graceland*

(a-wa) O kod wa u zo-nge li-sa namhlange
(a-wa a-wa) Si-bona kwenze ka kanjani
(a-wa a-wa) Amanto mbazane ayeza

She's a rich girl
She don't try to hide it
Diamonds on the soles of her shoes

He's a poor boy
Empty as a pocket
Empty as a pocket with nothing to lose
Sing, Ta na na
Ta na na na
She got diamonds on the soles of her shoes
Ta na na
Ta na na na
She got diamonds on the soles of her shoes
Diamonds on the soles of her shoes
Diamonds on the soles of her shoes
Diamonds on the soles of her shoes
Diamonds on the soles of her shoes

People say she's crazy
She got diamonds on the soles of her shoes
Well, that's one way to lose these
Walking blues
Diamonds on the soles of her shoes

She was physically forgotten
But then she slipped into my pocket
With my car keys
She said, "You've taken me for granted
Because I please you
Wearing these diamonds"

And I could say, Oo oo oo
As if everybody knows
What I'm talking about
As if everybody here would know
What I was talking about
Talking about diamonds on the soles of her shoes

She makes the sign of a teaspoon
He makes the sign of a wave
The poor boy changes clothes
And puts on aftershave
To compensate for his ordinary shoes

And she said, "Honey, take me dancing"
But they ended up by sleeping
In a doorway
By the bodegas and the lights on
Upper Broadway
Wearing diamonds on the soles of their shoes

And I could say, Oo oo oo
And everybody here would know
What I was talking about
I mean, everybody here would know exactly
What I was talking about
Talking about diamonds

People say I'm crazy
I got diamonds on the soles of my shoes, yeah
Well, that's one way to lose these
Walking blues
Diamonds on the soles of my shoes

(Beginning by Paul Simon and Joseph Shabalala)
From the album *Graceland*

A man walks down the street
He says, "Why am I soft in the middle now?
Why am I soft in the middle?
The rest of my life is so hard
I need a photo opportunity
I want a shot at redemption
Don't wanna end up a cartoon
In a cartoon graveyard"
Bonedigger, bonedigger
Dogs in the moonlight
Far away my well-lit door
Mr. Beerbelly, Beerbelly
Get these mutts away from me
You know I don't find this stuff
Amusing anymore

If you'll be my bodyguard
I can be your long-lost pal
I can call you Betty
And Betty, when you call me
You can call me Al

A man walks down the street
He says, "Why am I short of attention?
Got a short little span of attention
And, whoa, my nights are so long
Where's my wife and family?
What if I die here?
Who'll be my role model
Now that my role model is
Gone, gone?"
He ducked back down the alley
With some roly-poly little bat-faced girl
All along, along
There were incidents and accidents
There were hints and allegations

You Can Call Me Al

A man walks down the street
He says why am I soft in the middle now?
Why am I soft in the middle
When the rest of my life is so hard
I need a photo-opportunity
I want a shot at redemption
Don't want to end up a cartoon
In a graveyard
Bonedigger Bonedigger
Dogs in the moonlight.
Far away my well-lit door
Mr Beerbelly Beerbelly
take this child, Lord
Because we have no use for him

If you'll be my bodyguard
I could be your long-lost pal
I can call you Betty
and Betty when you call me
You can call me Al

A man walks down the street
He says Why am I short of attention
got a short little span of attention
and oh my nights are so long
Where's my wife and family
What if I die here
Who'll be my role-model
Now that my role-model is
Gone Gone
Ducked back in the alley
with some roly-poly little bat-faced woman
All along, along
There were incidents and accidents

If you'll be my bodyguard
I can be your long-lost pal
I can call you Betty
And Betty, when you call me
You can call me Al
Call me Al

A man walks down the street
It's a street in a strange world
Maybe it's the third world
Maybe it's his first time around
He doesn't speak the language
He holds no currency
He is a foreign man
He is surrounded by the sound, the sound
Cattle in the marketplace
Scatterlings and orphanages
He looks around, around
He sees angels in the architecture
Spinning in infinity
He says, "Amen!" and "Hallelujah!"

If you'll be my bodyguard
I can be your long-lost pal
I can call you Betty
And Betty, when you call me
You can call me Al
Call me

Na na na na . . .

If you'll be my bodyguard
I can call you Betty
If you'll be my bodyguard
I can call you Betty

From the album *Graceland*

Under African Skies (Duet)

Joseph's face was black as night
The pale yellow moon shone in his eyes
His path was marked
By the stars in the Southern Hemisphere
And he walked his days
Under African skies

This is the story of how we begin to remember
This is the powerful pulsing of love in the vein
After the dream of falling and calling your name out
These are the roots of rhythm
And the roots of rhythm remain

In early memory
Mission music
Was ringing 'round my nursery door
I said, "Take this child, Lord
From Tucson, Arizona
Give her the wings to fly through harmony
And she won't bother you no more"

This is the story of how we begin to remember
This is the powerful pulsing of love in the vein
After the dream of falling and calling your name out
These are the roots of rhythm
And the roots of rhythm remain

Joseph's face was as black as night
And the pale yellow moon shone in his eyes
His path was marked
By the stars in the Southern Hemisphere
And he walked the length of his days
Under African skies

From the album *Graceland*

Homeless

Emaweni webaba
Silale maweni
Webaba silale maweni

Webaba silale maweni
Webaba silale maweni
Webaba silale maweni

Webaba silale maweni
Webaba silale maweni
Webaba silale maweni
Webaba silale maweni
Webaba silale maweni

Homeless, homeless
Moonlight sleeping on a midnight lake
Homeless, homeless
Moonlight sleeping on a midnight lake
And we are homeless, we are homeless
The moonlight sleeping on a midnight lake
And we are homeless, homeless
The moonlight sleeping on a midnight lake

Zio yami, zio yami, nhliziyo yami
Nhliziyo yami amakhaza asengi bulele
Nhliziyo yami, nhliziyo yami
Nhliziyo yami, angibulele amakhaza
Nhliziyo yami, nhliziyo yami
Nhliziyo yami somandla angibulele mama
Zio yami, nhliziyo yami
Nhliziyo yami, nhliziyo yami

Too loo loo, too loo loo
Too loo loo loo loo loo loo loo loo loo
Too loo loo, too loo loo
Too loo loo loo loo loo loo loo loo loo

Strong wind destroy our home
Many dead, tonight it could be you
Strong wind, strong wind
Many dead, tonight it could be you

And we are homeless, homeless
Moonlight sleeping on a midnight lake
And we are homeless, homeless
Moonlight sleeping on a midnight lake
Homeless, homeless
Moonlight sleeping on a midnight lake

Somebody say ih hih ih hih ih
Somebody sing hello, hello, hello
Somebody say ih hih ih hih ih
Somebody cry why, why, why?
Somebody say ih hih ih hih ih
Somebody sing hello, hello, hello
Somebody say ih hih ih hih ih
Somebody cry why, why, why?
Somebody say ih hih ih hih ih

Yitho omanqoba (ih hih ih hih ih) yitho omanqoba
Esanqoba lonke ilizwe
(ih hih ih hih ih) Yitho omanqoba (ih hih ih hih ih)
Esanqoba phakathi e England

Yitho omanqoba
Esanqoba phakathi e London
Yitho omanqoba
Esanqoba phakathi e England

Somebody say ih hih ih hih ih
Somebody sing hello, hello, hello
Somebody say ih hih ih hih ih
Somebody cry why, why, why?
Somebody say ih hih ih hih ih
Somebody sing hello, hello, hello
Somebody say ih hih ih hih ih
Somebody cry why, why, why?

Kulumanani
Kulumani, Kulumani sizwe
Singenze njani
Baya jabula abasi thanda yo
Ho

(Words and music by Paul Simon and Joseph Shabalala)
From the album *Graceland*

Fat Charlie the Archangel
Sloped into the room
He said, "I have no opinion about this
And I have no opinion about that"
Sad as a lonely little wrinkled balloon
He said, "Well, I don't claim to be happy about this, boys
And I don't seem to be happy about that"

I don't want no part of this crazy love
I don't want no part of your love
I don't want no part of this crazy love
I don't want no part of your love
I don't want no part of this crazy love
I don't want no part of your love
I don't want no part of this crazy love
I don't want no part of this crazy love

She says she knows about jokes
This time the joke is on me
Well, I have no opinion about that
And I have no opinion about me

Somebody could walk into this room
And say, "Your life is on fire
It's all over the evening news
All about the fire in your life
On the evening news"

I don't want no part of this crazy love
I don't want no part of your love
I don't want no part of this crazy love
I don't want no part of your love

Fat Charlie the Archangel
Files for divorce
He says, "Well, this will eat up a year of my life
And then there's all that weight to be lost"
She says the joke is on me
I say the joke is on her
I said I have no opinion about that
Well, we'll just have to wait and confer

I don't want no part of this crazy love
I don't want no part of your love
I don't want no part of this crazy love
I don't want no part of your love

I don't want no part of this crazy love
I don't want no part of your love
I don't want no part of this crazy love

From the album *Graceland*

197

A long time ago, yeah
Before you was born, dude
When I was still single
And life was great
I held this job as a traveling salesman
That kept me moving from state to state

Well, I'm standing on the corner of Lafayette
State of Louisiana
Wondering where a city boy could go
To get a little conversation
Drink a little red wine
Catch a little bit of those Cajun girls
Dancing to zydeco

Along came a young girl
She's pretty as a prayer book
Sweet as an apple on Christmas Day
I said, "Good gracious, can this be my luck?
If that's my prayer book
Lord, let us pray"

198

Well, I'm standing on the corner of Lafayette
State of Louisiana
Wondering what a city boy could do
To get her in a conversation
Drink a little red wine
Dance to the music of Clifton Chenier
The King of the Bayou
'Et-toi!

Well, that was your mother
And that was your father
Before you was born, dude
When life was great
Now, you are the burden of my generation
I sure do love you
But let's get that straight

Well, I'm standing on the corner of Lafayette
Across the street from the Public
Heading down to the Lone Star Café
Maybe get a little conversation
Drink a little red wine
Standing in the shadow of Clifton Chenier
Dancing the night away

From the album *Graceland*

199

All Around the World
or
The Myth of Fingerprints

Over the mountain
Down in the valley
Lives a former talk-show host
Everybody knows his name
He says, "There's no doubt about it
It was the myth of fingerprints
I've seen them all and, man,
They're all the same"

Well, the sun gets weary
And the sun goes down
Ever since the watermelon
And the lights come up
On the black pit town
Somebody says, "What's a better thing to do?"
Well, it's not just me
And it's not just you
This is all around the world

Out in the Indian Ocean somewhere
There's a former army post
Abandoned now just like the war
And there is no doubt about it
It was the myth of fingerprints
That's what that old army post was for

Well, the sun gets bloody
And the sun goes down
Ever since the watermelon
And the lights come up
On the black pit town
Somebody says, "What's a better thing to do?"
Well, it's not just me
And it's not just you
This is all around the world

Over the mountain
Down in the valley
Lives the former talk-show host
Far and wide his name was known
He said, "There's no doubt about it
It was the myth of fingerprints
That's why we must learn to live alone"

Oo oo oo, live on
Live on
Live on
All around the world
All around the world

201

From the album *Graceland*

Changing Opinion

Gradually
We became aware
Of a hum in the room
An electrical hum in the room
It went mmmmmm

We followed it from
Corner to corner
We pressed our ears
Against the walls
We crossed diagonals
And put our hands on the floor
It went mmmmmm

Sometimes it was
A murmur
Sometimes it was
A pulse
Sometimes it seemed
To disappear
But then with a quarter turn
Of the head
It would roll around the sofa
A nimbus humming cloud
Mmmmmm

Maybe it's the hum
Of a calm refrigerator
Cooling on a big night
Maybe it's the hum
Of our parents' voices
Long ago in a soft light
Long ago in a dim light
Mmmmmm

Maybe it's the hum
Of changing opinion
Or a foreign language
In prayer
Maybe it's the mantra
Of the walls and wiring
Deep breathing
In soft air
Mmmmmm

From the album *Songs from Liquid Days*, by Philip Glass

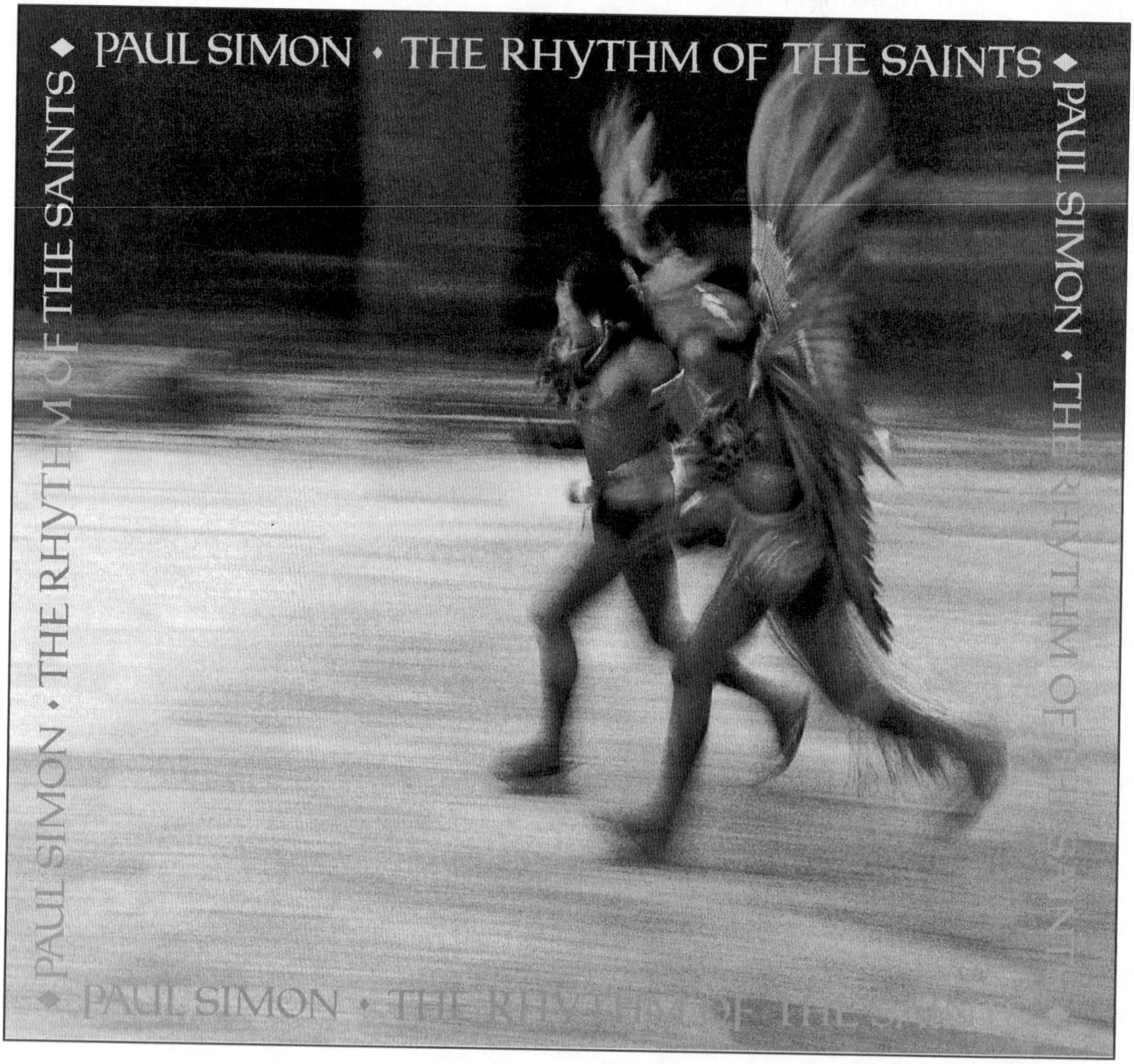

The Obvious Child

Well, I'm accustomed to a smooth ride
Or maybe I'm a dog who's lost its bite
I don't expect to be treated like a fool no more
I don't expect to sleep through the night
Some people say a lie's a lie's a lie
But I say why
Why deny the obvious child?
Why deny the obvious child?

And in remembering a road sign
I am remembering a girl when I was young
And we said, "These songs are true
These days are ours
These tears are free"
And hey
The cross is in the ballpark
The cross is in the ballpark

We had a lot of fun
We had a lot of money
We had a little son and we thought we'd call him Sonny
Sonny gets married and moves away
Sonny has a baby and bills to pay
Sonny gets sunnier
Day by day by day by day

Well, I've been waking up at sunrise
I've been following the light across my room
I watch the night receive the room of my day
Some people say the sky is just the sky
But I say
Why deny the obvious child?
Why deny the obvious child?

Sonny sits by his window and thinks to himself
How it's strange that some rooms are like cages
Sonny's yearbook from high school
Is down from the shelf
And he idly thumbs through the pages
Some have died
Some have fled from themselves
Or struggled from here to get there
Sonny wanders beyond his interior walls
Runs his hands through his thinning brown hair

Well, I'm accustomed to a smoother ride
Or maybe I'm a dog who's lost its bite
I don't expect to be treated like a fool no more
I don't expect to sleep the night
Some people say a lie is just a lie
But I say
The cross is in the ballpark
Why deny the obvious child?

From the album *The Rhythm of the Saints*

I can't run but
I can walk much faster than this
Can't run but
I can't run but
I can walk much faster than this
Can't run but

A cooling system
Burns out in the Ukraine
Trees and umbrellas
Protect us from the new rain
Armies of engineers
To analyze the soil
The food we contemplate
The water that we boil

I can't run but
I can walk much faster than this
Can't run but
I can't run but
I can walk much faster than this
Can't run but
Oo-wee Oo-wee

I had a dream about us
In the bottles and the bones of the night
I felt a pain in my shoulderblade
Like a pencil point? A love bite?
A couple was rubbing against us
Rubbing and doing that new dance
The man was wearing a jacket and jeans
The woman was laughing in advance

I can't run but
I can walk much faster than this
Can't run but
I can't run but
I can walk much faster than this
Cannot run but

A winding river
Gets wound around a heart
Pull it tighter and tighter
Until the muddy waters part
Down by the riverbank
A blues band arrives
The music suffers, baby
The music business thrives

I can't run but
I can walk much faster than this
Cannot run but
I can't run but
I can walk much faster than this
Cannot run but
Oo-wee Oo-wee

208

From the album *The Rhythm of the Saints*

A family of musicians took shelter for the night
In the little harbor church of St. Cecilia
Two guitars, batá, bass drum and tambourine
Rose of Jericho and bougainvillea

This is a lonely life
Sorrow's everywhere you turn
And that's worth something
When you think about it
That's worth some money
That's worth something
When you think about it
That is worth some money

A trip to the market
A trip into the pearl gray morning sunlight
That settles over Washington
A trip to the market
A trip around the world
Where the evening meal
Is negotiable, if there is one

This is a lonely-lone, lonely life
Sorrow's everywhere you turn
And that's worth something
When you think about it
That's worth some money
That's worth something
When you think about it
That is worth some money

To prove that I love you
Because I believe in you
Summer skies, stars are falling
And if I have money
If I have children
Summer skies, stars are falling
All along the injured coast
Oo-wah Oo-wah Doo-wop a Doo-wah
Summer skies and stars are falling
All along the injured coast
Oo-wah Oo-wah Doo-wop a Doo-wah
Summer skies, the stars are falling
All along the injured coast

We are standing in the sunlight
The early morning sunlight
In the harbor church of St. Cecilia
To praise a soul's returning to the earth
To the Rose of Jericho and the bougainvillea

This is the only life
And that's worth something
When you think about it
That is worth some money
That's worth something
When you think about it
That is worth some money

To prove that I love you
Because I believe in you
Summer skies, stars are falling
All along the injured coast
And if I have money
If I have children
Summer skies, stars are falling
All along the injured coast

If I have weaknesses
Don't let them blind me now
Summer skies, stars are falling
All along the injured coast
Oo-wah Oo-wah Doo-wop a Doo-wah
Summer skies, the stars are falling
Leaving the shadow of the valley behind me now
All along the injured coast
Oo-wah Oo-wah Doo-wop a Doo-wah
Summer skies, the stars are falling
All along the injured coast
Oo-wah Oo-wah Doo-wop a Doo-wah

211

From the album *The Rhythm of the Saints*

Soon our fortunes will be made, my darling
And we will leave this loathsome little town
Silver bells jingling from your black lizard boots, my baby
Silver foil to trim your wedding gown

It's true, the tools of love wear down
Time passes
A mind wanders
It seems mindless, but it does
Sometimes I see your face
As if through reading glasses
And your smile, it seems softer than it was

Proof
Some people gonna call you up
Tell you something that you already know
Proof
Sane people go crazy on you
Say, "No, man, that's not
The deal we made
I got to go, I got to go"
Faith
Faith is an island in the setting sun
But proof, yes
Proof is the bottom line for everyone

My face, my race
Don't matter anymore
My sex, my checks
Accepted at the door

Proof
Some people gonna call you up
Tell you something that you already know
Proof
Sane people go crazy on you
Say, "No, man, that's not
The deal we made
I got to, I got to go"
Faith
Faith is an island in the setting sun
But proof, yes
Proof is the bottom line for everyone

Half moon hiding in the clouds, my darling
And the sky is flecked with signs of hope
Raise your weary wings against the rain, my baby
Wash your tangled curls with gambler's soap

Proof
Some people gonna call you up
Tell you something that you already know
Proof
Sane people go crazy on you
Say, "No, man, that's not
The deal we made
I got to, I got to, I got to"
Faith
Faith is an island in the setting sun
But proof, yes
Proof is the bottom line for everyone
But proof, yes
Proof is the bottom line for everyone

From the album *The Rhythm of the Saints*

There may come a time
When you'll be tired
As tired as a dream that wants to die
Further to fly
Further to fly
Further to fly
Further to fly

Maybe you will find a love
That you discover accidentally
Who falls against you gently as
A pickpocket brushes your thigh
Further to fly

Effortless music from the Cameroons
The spinning darkness of her hair
A conversation in a crowded room going nowhere
The open palm of desire
Wants everything
It wants everything
It wants everything

Sometimes I'll be walking down
The street and I'll be thinking
Am I crazy
Or is this some morbid little lie?
Further to fly
Further to fly
Further to fly

A recent loss of memory
A shadow in the family
The baby waves bye-bye
I'm trying
I'm flying

There may come a time
When I will lose you
Lose you as I lose my light
Days falling backward into velvet night
The open palm of desire
Wants everything
It wants everything
It wants soil as soft as summer
And the strength to push like spring

A broken laugh, a broken fever
Take it up with the great deceiver
Who looks you in the eye
Says, Baby, don't cry
Further to fly

There may come a time
When I will lose you
Lose you as I lose my sight
Days falling backward into velvet night
The open palm of desire
The Rose of Jericho
Soil as soft as summer
The strength to let you go

215

From the album *The Rhythm of the Saints*

I feel good
It's a fine day
The way the sun hits off the runway
A cloud shifts
The plane lifts
She moves on

But feel the bite
Whenever you believe that
You'll be lost and love will find you
When the road bends
And the song ends
She moves on

I know the reason
I feel so blessed
My heart still splashes
Inside my chest, but she
She is like a top
She cannot stop
She moves on

A sympathetic stranger
Lights a candle in the middle of the night
Her voice cracks
She jumps back
But she moves on, moves on

She says, "Ooh, my storybook lover
You have underestimated my power
As you shortly will discover"

Then I fall to my knees
Shake a rattle at the skies
And I'm afraid that I'll be taken
Abandoned, forsaken
In her cold coffee eyes

She can't sleep now
The moon is red
She fights a fever
She burns in bed
She needs to talk so
We take a walk
Down in the moonlight

She says, "Maybe these emotions are
As near to love as love will ever be"
So I agree
Then the moon breaks
She takes the corner, that's all she takes
She moves on

She says, "Ooh, my storybook lover
You have underestimated my power
As you shortly will discover"

Then I fall to my knees
I grow weak, I go slack
As if she captured the breath of my
Voice in a bottle
And I can't catch it back

But I feel good
It's a fine day
The way the sun hits off the runway
A cloud shifts
The plane lifts
She moves on

217

From the album *The Rhythm of the Saints*

Down among the reeds and rushes
A baby boy was found
His eyes as clear as centuries
His silky hair was brown

Never been lonely
Never been lied to
Never had to scuffle in fear
Nothing denied to
Born at the instant
The church bells chime
The whole world whispering
Born at the right time

Me and my buddies, we are traveling people
We like to go down to Restaurant Row
Spend those Eurodollars
All the way from Washington to Tokyo
Well, I see them in the airport lounges
Upon their mother's breast
They follow me with open eyes
Their uninvited guest

Never been lonely
Never been lied to
Never had to scuffle in fear
Nothing denied to
Born at the instant
The church bells chime
And the whole world whispering
Born at the right time

There's too many people on the bus from the airport
Too many holes in the crust of the earth
The planet groans
Every time it registers another birth

But down among the reeds and rushes
A baby girl was found
Her eyes as clear as centuries
Her silky hair was brown
Never been lonely
Never been lied to
Never had to scuffle in fear
Nothing denied to
Born at the instant
The church bells chime
And the whole world whispering
Born at the right time

From the album *The Rhythm of the Saints*

The Cool, Cool River

Moves like a fist through traffic
Anger and no one can heal it
Shoves a little bump into the momentum
It's just a little lump
But you feel it
In the creases and the shadows
With a rattling, deep emotion
The cool, cool river
Sweeps the wild, white ocean

Yes, Boss—the government handshake
Yes, Boss—the crusher of language
Yes, Boss—Mr. Stillwater
The face at the edge of the banquet
The cool, the cool river
The cool, the cool river

I believe in the future
I may live in my car
My radio tuned to
The voice of a star
Song dogs barking at the break of dawn
Lightning pushes the edge of a thunderstorm
And these old hopes and fears
Still at my side

Anger and no one can heal it
Slides through the metal detector
Lives like a mole in a motel
A slide in a slide projector
The cool, cool river
Sweeps the wild, white ocean
The rage, the rage of love turns inward
To become prayers of devotion
And these prayers are
The constant road across the wilderness
These prayers are
These prayers are the memory of God
The memory of God

And I believe in the future
We shall suffer no more
Maybe not in my lifetime
But in yours, I feel sure
Song dogs barking at the break of dawn
Lightning pushes the edges of a thunderstorm
And these streets
Quiet as a sleeping army
Send their battered dreams to heaven, to heaven
For the mother's restless son
Who is a witness to, who is a warrior
Who denies his urge to break and run

Who says, "Hard times?
I'm used to them
The speeding planet burns
I'm used to that
My life's so common it disappears"
And sometimes even music
Cannot substitute for tears

From the album *The Rhythm of the Saints*

221

Spirit Voices

We sailed up a river wide as a sea
And slept on the banks
On the leaves of a banyan tree
And all of these spirit voices rule the night

Some stories are magical, meant to be sung
Songs from the mouth of the river
When the world was young
And all of these spirit voices rule the night

By moon
We walk
To the brujo's door
Along a path of river stones
Women with their nursing children
Seated on the floor
We join the fevers
And the broken bones

The candlelight flickers
The falcon calls
A lime green lizard scuttles down the cabin wall
And all of these spirit voices
Sing rainwater, seawater
River water, holy water
Wrap this child in mercy—heal her
Heaven's only daughter
All of these spirit voices rule the night

My hands were numb
And my feet were lead
I drank a cup of herbal brew
Then the sweetness in the air
Combined with the lightness in my head
And I heard the jungle breathing in the bamboo

Saudocões	Greetings!
Da licenca un momento	Excuse me, one moment
Te lembró	I remind you
Que amanhã	That tomorrow
Será tudo ou será naoa	It will be all or it will be nothing
Depende coração	It depends, heart
Será breve ou será grande	It will be brief or it will be great
Depende da paixão	It depends on the passion
Será sujo, será sonho	It will be dirty, it will be a dream
Cuidado, coração	Be careful, heart
Será útil, será tarde	It will be useful, it will be late
Se esmera, coração	Do your best, heart
E confia	And have trust
Na força do amanhã	In the power of tomorrow

The Lord of the earthquake
My trembling bed
The spider resumes the rhythm
Of its golden thread
And all of these spirit voices rule the night
And all of these spirit voices rule the night
And all of these spirit voices rule the night

223

From the album *The Rhythm of the Saints*

If I have weaknesses
Don't let them blind me
Or camouflage all I am wary of
I could be sailing on seizures of laughter
Or crawling out from under the heel of love
Do my prayers remain unanswered
Like a beggar at your sleeve?
Olodumare is smiling in heaven
Smiling in heaven, I do believe

Reach in the darkness
A reach in the dark
Reach in the darkness
A reach in the dark
To overcome an obstacle or an enemy
To glide away from the razor or a knife
To overcome an obstacle or an enemy
To dominate the impossible in your life

Always a stranger when strange isn't fashionable
And fashion is rich people waving at the door
Or it's a dealer in drugs or in passion
Lies of a nature we've heard before
Do my prayers remain unanswered
Like a beggar at your sleeve?
Babalu-aye spins on his crutches
Says, "Leave if you want
If you want to leave"

Reach in the darkness
A reach in the dark
Reach in the darkness
A reach in the dark
To overcome an obstacle or an enemy
To glide away from the razor or a knife
To overcome an obstacle or an enemy
To dominate the impossible in your life
Reach in the darkness
A reach in the dark
Reach in the darkness
A reach in the dark
To overcome an obstacle or an enemy
To dominate the impossible in your life
Reach in the darkness
A reach in the dark
Reach in the darkness
A reach in the dark

From the album *The Rhythm of the Saints*

Thelma

If a baby is born and no one complains
Then it's good luck runnin' through young veins
And if life is a blessing
That brushes the tops of the trees
Well, it's a short walk in a sweet breeze

I will need you, feed you
Seed you, plead with you
Beg you not to leave me alone
All for a taste of your sweet love, Thelma

If the heart is an open memory book
That was the chance I took
The more I searched
The more I shook for Thelma

Last night I slept on a rented pillow
A silver moon above my head
A thirsty dreamless sleep released me
And I reached for the phone by the side of the bed

Now, the first time that I saw you I thought
She's beautiful, but she's too young to be caught
People aware of my history
Trying to steer you away from me
I left a message at your hotel
Don't let management poison the well

I will need you, feed you
Seed you, plead with you
All for a taste of your sweet love, Thelma

The phone is ringing and I realize
We are time zones and oceans apart
The words I speak in the middle of my night
Fall on your yesterday's heart

If the sun don't shine
If the wind don't break
If the clock don't jump off the wall
Thelma, my darlin', I will cushion your fall

I will need you, feed you
Seed you, plead with you
Without the taste of your sweet love, Thelma

I am only a man who skirted the edge of despair
For a long time now
And I don't care
I watch you sleeping in the hospital bed
The baby curled up in a ball
Winter sunlight hits the family tree
And everything else becomes nothing at all

227

From the box set *Paul Simon 1964–1993*

You are moving on a crowded street
Through various shades of people
In the summer's harshest heat
A story in your eye

Well, speak until your mind is at ease

Ten years come and gone so fast
I might as well have been dreaming
Sunny days have burned a path
Across another season

A fortune rises to the sky

Ten years come and gone so fast
I might as well have been dreaming

You are driving down an empty road
Beside a shady river
When the sky turns dark as stone
And the trees begin to shiver

The grace of God is nigh

Ten years come and gone
And that flash has never been forgotten
Sunny days have burned a path
Across another season

How do the powerless survive?

Ten years come and gone so fast
I might as well have been dreaming

228

If you look into your future life
Ten years from this question
Do you imagine a familiar light
Burning in the distance?

The love that never dies
Ten years come and gone so fast
I might as well have been dreaming
Sunny days have burned a path
Across another season

Ten years come and gone so fast
Sunny days have burned a path

1991-1998

The Capeman
Lyrics by Paul Simon
and Derek Walcott

El Coquíto
Born in Puerto Rico
In Mayagüez
Carmen
Santero
Chimes
Christmas in the Mountains
Satin Summer Nights
Bernadette
The Vampires
Shopliftin' Clothes
Dance to a Dream
Quality
Manhunt (Run, Spic, Run)
Can I Forgive Him?
Adios Hermanos
Jesús Es Mi Señor

Sunday Afternoon
Time Is an Ocean
Wahzinak's First Letter
Killer Wants to Go to College
Virgil
Wahzinak's Duet
My Only Defense
Virgil & the Warden
Trailways Bus
El Malecón
You Fucked Up My Life
Lazarus/Last Drop of Blood
Wahzinak's Last Letter
Puerto Rican Day Parade
El Coquí (Reprise)
Tony Hernandez
Carlos & Yolanda
Sal's Last Song
Esmeralda's Dream

El Coquíto (Little Tree Toad—Puerto Rican Folk Song) (Olcutt Sanders)

CHILDREN (OFFSTAGE)

Êl co-quí, el co-quí a mi me encanta
Es tan lindo el cantar del coquí
Por las noches al ir a acostarme
Me a-dor-me-ce can-tan-do a-si
Co-quí, co-quí, co-quí, quí, quí, quí!
Co-quí, co-quí, co-quí, quí, quí, quí!

SALVADOR

Mama, it's Sal
I'm almost there
I'm safe and my spirit is unbroken
I've tasted my first breath of freedom's air
But there's the truth that still needs to be spoken

From *The Capeman*

233

SALVADOR

I was born in Puerto Rico
Came here when I was a child
Before I reached the age of sixteen
I was running with a gang and we were wild

I see myself those summer evenings
Hanging out with boys from Lexington and Park
Red beans and rice from kitchen windows
It's suppertime and the *Barrio* is dark
No one knows you like I do
Nobody can know your heart the way I do
No one can testify to all that you've been through
But I will

SAL AND THE VAMPIRES

I was born in Puerto Rico
And my blood is *taino*
Spanish Caribbean in my soul

234

SALVADOR

We came here wearing summer clothes in winter
Hearts of sunshine in the cold
Your family rented this apartment
You'd watch the streetlamps from your perch
In the sacramental hour your stepfather in black
Preached the fire of the Pentecostal Church
No one knows you like I do
Nobody can know your heart the way I do
No one can testify to all that you've been through
But this will

SAL AND THE VAMPIRES

I was born in Puerto Rico
Came here when I was a child

SALVADOR

Small change and sunlight, then I left these streets for good
My days as short as they were wild

CARLOS APACHE

I'm Carlos Apache

ANGEL SOTO

Angel Soto

FRENCHY CORDERO

Frenchy Cordero

BABU CHARLIE CRUZ

Babu Charlie Cruz

235

TONY HERNANDEZ

Tony Hernandez

SAL AND SALVADOR

Salvador Agrón

SALVADOR

Your faces blurred in every grainy photo
And fading headline of the *Daily News*

One year Wiltwyck School for Criminal Children
Three years Auburn, one year Brooklyn House of D.
Eight years Dannemora, one year Sing Sing, one year Attica
Five years Greenhaven
Twenty years inside, today we're free
You cannot even read your story
The pages piling up in shame
Before the words release you, the guard will kill the light
The night you took The Capeman for your name

CHORUS AND SALVADOR

I was born in Puerto Rico
I was born in Puerto Rico

THE VAMPIRES

I was born in Puerto Rico
I was born in Puerto Rico
I was born in Puerto Rico
I was born in Puerto Rico
I was born in Puerto Rico
I was born in Puerto Rico

From *The Capeman*

In Mayagüez

SALVADOR

In Mayagüez, a mountain town
Along the western shore
We saw the roofs as we came down
To the asylum for the poor

The sugarcane whispered its prayers
And laid them on the sea
El Asilo de los Pobres
Is where our home will be

CHILDREN AND NUNS

Pray for us, Santa Maria
Stay with us, Salvador
Pray for us, Santa Maria
Stay with us, Salvador

SALVADOR

My mother, Esmeralda
Worked in the kitchen as a maid
While I played games with the crazy ones
In the Flamboyan's light and shade

FIRST NUN

Your mother named you for our Lord
But you cry, you wet your bed

SECOND NUN

This filthy habit must be cured

THIRD NUN

Look how the stain has spread

CHILDREN

El meón, el meón
Se mojó el pantalón
El meón, el meón

El meón, el meón
Se mojó el pantalón
El meón, el meón

THREE NUNS

We only tried to train the boy

ESMERALDA

You're animals at heart!

THREE NUNS

You've had our charity to enjoy

ESMERALDA

We'll make another start
There was a crucifixion, yes
But this time it is my son
This time it is not you, Jesus
But Salvador Agrón

SALVADOR

A dirt road leads to heaven
Through the canes in Mayagüez
I walked it, I was seven
She watered it with tears

CHILDREN AND NUNS

Pray for us, Santa Maria
Stay with us, Salvador
Pray for us, Santa Maria
Stay with us, Salvador

From *The Capeman*

Carmen

CARMEN

My God, what happened?

ESMERALDA

The Sisters of Charity punished him

CARMEN

They call them mothers
But they have no children
Some cream of aloes will soothe his skin
My name is Carmen
Are you their mother?
Such lovely innocents
What were they christened?

ESMERALDA

This one is Aurea
The boy is Salvador

CARMEN

Salve for little Salvi
This will burn

240

ESMERALDA

What will I do?
I don't know what to do
Where to turn
I feel like everything
That happens is my fault
These are my wealth
Where is the money? I must turn
I see my children, and my eyes are filled with salt

CARMEN

Go to the santero
My life was uncertain
Sometimes we need to see behind the curtain
When you come to the end of
The Santa Cruz Road
There's a path across the meadow
A fence of cactus high
Is the painted house of the santero
All he asks is that you trust him
And the shells he will throw

241

From *The Capeman*

Santero

CHANTER

Bara súwà yo omo yàl àwà'nà yo
Màmà kè'ní ir'awo-e
O bara wà yo ekè èsú òdàrà omo yàl àwà'nà
Màmà kè'ní ir'awo-e

CELEBRANTS CHORUS

Bara súwà yo omo yàl àwà'nà
Màmà kè'ní ir'awo-e
O bara su wà yo ekè èsú òdàrà omo yàl àwà'nà
Màmà kè'ní ir'awo-e

ESMERALDA

I am Esmeralda, I worked at *el asilo*
Today I quit
Now we have no place to go
But a woman from the *botanica*
The one whose name is Carmen
Said in times of need
You interpret any omen
I almost used a knife today
I could have killed someone
Will this cast a shadow on my son?

242

SANTERO

In New York, on a hot night
There's a playground filled with cries
As a quarter moon like a dagger
Tears across the sky
So say the shells
So say the shells

Elegua, king of the crossroads
His colors red and black
Sees a blade leap in the moonlight
But he does not hold it back
So say the shells
Ma fere fun los caracoles

ESMERALDA

I know my son is mischievous
Maybe troublesome, not wicked
Why should his feet obey the path
A few shells have predicted?

I don't believe in spirits
I have no superstition
But I've given you my money
Finish your prediction
Throw the shells

243

SANTERO

I see him staggering through the desert
But he must not break his chain
Till Saint Lazarus in his mercy
Turns his thirsty soul to rain
So say the shells
Ma fere fun los caracoles

SANTERO AND LAZARUS

So this, then, is the future
From which no one can escape
The cape and the umbrella
The umbrella and the cape
So say the shells

LAZARUS

Ma fere fun los caracoles

SANTERO AND LAZARUS

So say the shells

LAZARUS

Ma fere fun los caracoles

SANTERO AND LAZARUS

So say the shells

SANTERO

So say the shells

From *The Capeman*

244

Chimes

Salvador, my Salvador
What have I done?
I have only myself to blame
I should have known the shells would fall
And make a mockery of your name
How could I trust a man
Who can read the cards like prophecies?
Or roll the stars like dice
And turn a simple woman's savings
Into a gambler's pack of lies?

Lies that shatter her heart like crystal
And pound her heart like a drum
At the shape in those predictions
Of what you will become

Listen to the children singing, Salvi
Listen to the poorhouse bells
See the supper they are bringing
To their mouths like little shells

245

I'd wash all the laundry of the ocean
I'd scrub all the poorhouse floors
To stop the moon in motion
From the fate he said is yours
How could anyone look into your eyes, such pure eyes
And see a murderer in there?
I see an angel on a hillside
With moonlight in his hair
I hear the voices in the sea
They say the stars will be our city lights
Your soul is safe with me
Our roots are here in Mayagüez
The santero's words are strong
But he read the fate of someone else
The prophecy is wrong

From *The Capeman*

CHORUS

It is Christmas in the mountains
The air is cool and brighter
And the blossoms of the plantains
Make my sorrows lighter

SINGER

We are not the three kings
But musicians, and the gift we bring
Is neither gold nor frankincense
But the Aguinaldo we sing

And the wine and cake we play for
We know you'll want to share them
In the name of our Savior
Born this day in Bethlehem

CARMEN

What did he say, the santero?

ESMERALDA

It was bad news, and then it got worse

247

CARMEN

I'm so sorry that I sent you
What did he say that hurt?

ESMERALDA

Some nonsense about Lazarus
And wandering in the desert

CARMEN

What now, Esmeralda?
What's in store for you?

ESMERALDA

I don't shop in any store
That makes a crazy woman out of you

NEIGHBOR

Esmeralda, Esmeralda
The new postman is drunk
This package comes from New York
It's addressed to you, I think
From a Reverend Gonzalez
I examined it in detail

SECOND NEIGHBOR

Don't you know it's a federal offense
To read your neighbor's mail?

ESMERALDA

Ay, Dios mio
If I weren't scared, I'd laugh
The cape he said was red and black
The colors of this scarf
A ticket for New York
He wants me for his wife

CARMEN

You cannot live in constant fear
You have to change your life

It is Christmas in the mountains
The air is cool and brighter
And the blossoms of the plantains
Make my sorrows lighter

248

ESMERALDA

After Gumersindo left me
So treacherous and handsome
I had no one to protect me
Or look after my small ones
Then, with Reverend Gonzalez
I spoke about my son
He was going back to America
Said he'd send for us soon

CARMEN

Don't you fear the santero's prediction?

ESMERALDA

I am not a woman of stone
A hawk in the sky is crying
You were not meant to live alone

CHORUS

It is Christmas in the mountains
The air is cool and brighter
And the blossoms of the plantains
Make my sorrows lighter

249

ENSEMBLE

And no matter where you may go
And you may be gone for years
When you hear the Aguinaldo
Remember Mayagüez

From *The Capeman*

Satin Summer Nights

S AL

I've been sleeping on the roof of my building
It's cooler than the street
And I been watching the setting sun
As it bounces off the avenue
Turning into gold dust at my feet
Woh-oo-woh
Carlos and Yolanda
Dancing in the hallway
To an old melody
Spanish eyes and soft brown curls
My love, my love
Come to me

I believe I'm in the power of Saint Lazarus
And he holds me in his sight
I know that these jitterbug days I'm living
Well, they won't last for all of us
But they'll last for a long summer night
Woh-o-woh
I can feel the fire in her eyes
Tonight, tonight
Under satin summer skies

B ERNADETTE

Baby, baby, baby
Be my special one
I seen you move in from across the street
I like the way you walk
I love the way you run

YOLANDA

Baby, baby
No more baby talk

BERNADETTE

Baby, baby
Papi, this ain't Mayagüez

BERNADETTE AND YOLANDA

This is the island of *Nueva York*

BERNADETTE

We'll go through the projects

BERNADETTE AND YOLANDA

Make-out on the roof

BERNADETTE

251

Count the stars like silver studs

BERNADETTE AND YOLANDA

On my motorcycle boots

UMBRELLA MAN

You wastin' your time
They don't know what I do
You little ghetto weeds
I feel like killin' you
Boo!

Banana-colored light-skinned spics
You feel your peel so fine
I'm Hernandez, the Umbrella Man
Your future's locked in mine
The Chaplains and the Golden Guineas
The Red Wings and the Crowns
The mighty Mau Maus, those shines from Brooklyn
They want to cut the Vampires down
The Savage Skulls, the Fordham Baldies
They treat you like you're piss
From the heart of the *Barrio*, now, my brother
We tell them motherfuckers, "Suck on this"

I think we got something to talk about
You're a coolie from the turf
That's cool, but you don't get no respect around here unless
You belong to a bopping gang
You either belong or you get hurt
Or you can buy some protection from me

'Cause if someone's got to die
To pay for the shit they done
I believe in an eye for an eye
What you believe in, Salvador Agrón?
Mr. Agrón, Señor Agrón

S A L

I believe I'm in the power of Saint Lazarus
And he holds me in his sight
I believe he watches over us all
Don't tear apart
This satin summer night

F r o m   *The Capeman*

Bernadette

Whoa—I got time on my hands tonight
You're the girl of my dreams
When I'm near you, my future seems bright
I want you to be my girl
I want you to be my movie
I am Sal Mineo, and I need you so

Whoa—you got style from your hair to your heels
Though my words may be jumbled
Still, I'm telling you just how it feels
I love you

Sal and Bernadette

I love you
And the breeze that wraps around you

Sal

Satin summer nights

253

Sal and Bernadette

A night I can't forget

Sal

Whoa—you're the smile of the moon, Bernadette

Doo-Wop

Dom dom dom zoom
Well-a well, I'm home
Dom dom dom zoom
Well-a well, I'm home

DOO-WOP

Wop, wop, wop, wop, wop

SAL AND DOO-WOP

Come with me
There's a place I want you to see

When the leaves are dark
I've got a hiding place in Central Park

SAL

And the sky is a coat of diamonds

There's a wooden cross over my bed
The city is lit with candles
They're shining for you, Bernadette

Whoa—you're the smile of the moon

SAL AND DOO-WOP

Dom dom dom zoom
Well-a well, I'm home
Dom dom dom zoom
Well-a well, I'm home

DOO-WOP

Wop, wop, wop, wop, wop

From *The Capeman*

The Vampires

HERNANDEZ

I see the Red Wings worked you over real good
You don't walk across another neighborhood

SAL

Just don't touch me, alright?

HERNANDEZ

Oh, now you ready to rumble?
I'm scared!
I'm gonna run to your stepfather's church and start praying
Oye, motherfucker, where's this *Jibaro* from?
You know it takes a strong man to survive

HERNANDEZ AND BABU CHARLIE CRUZ

It ain't no accident that you're still alive

HERNANDEZ, VAMPIRES AND DOO-WOP

We stand for the neighborhood

255

HERNANDEZ

He still lives with his mami, but he sneaks down
A coolie in the shadow of the playground
You want to fight for your people—don't you, Sal?

SAL

If I got to

HERNANDEZ

Oh, you got to. Believe me
Come here, man, I want to show you something
Ven pa' cá

This is the cave of the Vampires
Count Dracula's castle
The very sight could turn a white man gray
Made in the shade, use my umbrella
Black like the night we fly in
That blade is all you need
To keep the dogs away

So you gonna be a Vampire, man! That's good
We always looking for young blood in the neighborhood
Carlos Apache collects the dues
So you bring us something that we can use

HERNANDEZ AND VAMPIRES

If you got the balls, then come on, *mete mano*

BABU CHARLIE CRUZ

Vaya Carlos!

HERNANDEZ AND VAMPIRES

If you got the balls, then come on, *mete mano*

HERNANDEZ

Frenchy Cordero goes down to Hell's Kitchen
To sell the Irish some weed
This Paddy Boy's mother on the stoop starts bitchin'
'Bout "Spics is a mongrel breed"
Now here comes her son
He looks like a ton of corned beef
Floating in beer
He says
"Fucking Puerto Rican dope-dealing punks
Get your shit-brown ass out of here!"

HERNANDEZ AND VAMPIRES

He said
"Fucking Puerto Rican dope-dealing punk
Get your shit-brown ass out of here!"
Yeah, yeah

HERNANDEZ

These shantytown Irish kicked his ass good
And they fractured his collarbone
Coño, all I was thinking, "What home of the brave?
This is a fucking war zone"

VAMPIRES

If you got the balls, then come on, *mete mano*
If you got cojones, come on, *mete mano*
If you got the balls, then come on, *mete mano*
If you got cojones, come on, *mete mano*

Mete mano
Mete mano
Mete mano

257

From *The Capeman*

Shopliftin' Clothes

SAL, HERNANDEZ AND VAMPIRES

Well, I believe it's that time of year
When I shop for clothes
Well, I believe it's that time of year
When I shop for clothes
It tells you how far your hard-earned money goes

SALESWOMAN

Come on in, boys, get yourself a better view
Have a look around, see if anything appeals to you
We got a sale right now

SALESMAN

You buy one, you get two

SALESWOMAN (TO HERNANDEZ)

258

Just look at the way that fabric drapes your leg
Now imagine that with a saddle stitch
And a twelve-inch peg
Women see you coming
They'll get down on their knees and beg

SAL, HERNANDEZ AND VAMPIRES

Well, I believe it's that time of year
When I shop for clothes
Well, I believe it's that time of year
When I shop for clothes
Tells you how far your hard-earned money goes

S ALESMAN

We're featuring the Ivy League look
It's conservative

S ALESWOMAN

But cool

S ALESMAN

And with a "Mr. B" collar
Now you're breaking all the rules
Well, how about a sharkskin suit?
Shines just like a jewel

S ALESWOMAN

If it's a hat you require
Let me show you one of our stingy brims
Here, check yourself out in the mirror
This shipment just come in

S ALESMAN

Man! That hat is you

S ALESWOMAN

That hat is him

S ALESMAN (TO **S** AL)

Sorry, my man, but the cape is not for sale
I got a shipment coming in any day now
Via the air mail
Yeah, this item is gonna be very fashionable
Come the fall

SAL, HERNANDEZ AND VAMPIRES

Well, I believe it's that time of year
When I shop for clothes
Well, I believe it's that time of year
When I shop for clothes
It tells you how far your hard-earned money goes

From *The Capeman*

Dance to a Dream

CARLOS

Come on, Yolanda, I just wanna see

YOLANDA

Carlos, not here! What, are you crazy?

CARLOS

You know I love you
They all know I love you, too, so?

YOLANDA

So what we do together is private
You can dance to the dream of a summer night
As you drift to the edge of desire

CARLOS AND YOLANDA

Guided by love's mysterious light
To the stars in heaven on fire

261

YOLANDA

Uh-huh

BERNADETTE

Uh-huh

YOLANDA

Uh-huh

BERNADETTE

Uh-huh

YOLANDA

I have always imagined a better life
Far from the *Barrio's* gutters
We could manage a club as a husband and wife
Build a house, paint the shutters

CARLOS, YOLANDA AND BERNADETTE

You can dance to the dream of a summer night
As you drift to the edge of desire
Guided by love's mysterious light

CARLOS, YOLANDA, BERNADETTE AND SAL

262   To the stars in heaven on fire

SAL

Hey, Bernadette, what you wanna bet
I can fly like the guys in the comic books?
You know how magic this cape is

BERNADETTE

I'll be your nurse, and wherever it hurts
I'll bandage your wounds with my kisses

YOLANDA

Uh-huh

BERNADETTE

Uh-huh

YOLANDA

Uh-huh

BERNADETTE

Uh-huh

YOLANDA

A restaurant, white tablecloths
And maybe some live Spanish music
Search for our dreams, sometimes they're lost
But it's my dream and I don't want to lose it

CARLOS, YOLANDA AND BERNADETTE

You can dance to the dream of a summer night
As you drift to the edge of desire
Guided by love's mysterious light

263

CARLOS, YOLANDA, BERNADETTE AND SAL

To the stars in heaven on fire

YOLANDA

There are lawns and flowers on a Westchester street
Maples that sound like a river

CARLOS

A place for our children that's restful and sweet
I promise you, one day we'll live there

CARLOS, YOLANDA AND BERNADETTE

You can dance to the dream of a summer night
As we drift to the edge of desire
Guided by love's mysterious light
To the stars in heaven on fire

From *The Capeman*

264

Quality

SAL

The way you move
It's got quality

Come on, baby, let's go downtown
Little girl, you sure look good to me
The way you move
It's got quality

Come on, baby, now don't be shy
Step in the light so I can see
The way you move
It's got quality

BERNADETTE AND YOLANDA

I want to know
Are you my beautiful young boy?
Or just another love
Passing through my life?
I need to know
Will you be my sorrow and my joy?
And maybe one day soon
Will I be your wife?

SAL

Come on, baby, let's rock some more
I want to spend my salary
The way you move
It's got quality

Zoom zoom zoom zoom
Every time they see me
Walk down the street, they say
"*Coño*, that boy is fine
The way he moves
It's got quality"

BERNADETTE AND YOLANDA

I want to know
Are you my beautiful young boy?
Or just another love
Passing through my life?
I need to know
Will you be my sorrow and my joy?
And maybe one day soon
Will I be your wife?

SALVADOR

Who can stop the setting sun
Or who can raise the dead?
I feel the shame of what was done
See how the stain has spread

SAL

Come on, baby, let's go downtown
Little girl, you sure look good to me
The way you move
It's got quality
The way you move
It's got quality

From *The Capeman*

Manhunt (Run, Spic, Run)

SALVADOR

I hear the wailing sirens cry
I jostle through the crowd
I see two bodies lifted high
As angels in their shroud

CABDRIVER

My name is Willie Carter
And I drive a yellow cab
I picked up them Puerto Ricans
About 12:15 A.M.
On the corner of Forty-sixth Street
I ain't like the looks of them
They wanted me to drop 'em up on
San Juan Hill
The little guy with the stingy brim
Looked mean enough to kill

267

CHORUS

Run, spic, run from the shadow of the law
Run, boy, run—you're the one they're searching for

REPORTER

The mayor of New York, Robert F. Wagner

"There's no parental guidance
And the courts will share the blame
Leniency for animals that lead a life of crime
The city is sick of this violence
The people have taken a stand
I've asked Police Commissioner Kennedy for fourteen hundred men"

CHORUS

Run, spic, run from the shadow of the law
Run, boy, run—you're the one they're searching for

COP

You were at the scene of the murder

CARLOS

Yeah, but I did not use a knife

COP

So tell us who the killer is

CARLOS

Man, he's runnin' for his life

REPORTER

A little bit more of this conversation
And the killer's name was known
He's sixteen-year-old Puerto Rican Salvador Agrón

268

SALVADOR

Afraid for our lives, we vanished in the Bronx
Taking food from garbage
And hiding from the light

COP

Hey, hold it right there. What'd ya drop?
Pick it up. Yeah, bring it over here
Unwrap it. Let me see it. What the fuck is this?
Yeah, step into the light. Let me get a better look at your face

SAL

Yeah, I'm the one you're looking for, copper
I'm the one who used the knife

COP

Hey, Paddy, get over here—take a look at this
Yeah, I think we got the Capeman!

269

CHORUS (GROWING IN NUMBER)

Kill the spics!
Kill the spics!
Kill the spics!

AUREA

Our mother brought a Bible
But the word of the Lord was spurned

SAL

I don't care if they fry me
My mother could watch me burn

ARRESTING OFFICERS (SPOKEN)

We got a shitload of reporters out there

SECOND COP

Yeah, that guy from Channel Four is here with a TV crew. Let's go

Run, spic, run
Run, spic, run
Run, spic, run
Run, spic, run

From *The Capeman*

270

Can I Forgive Him?

ESMERALDA

I am Esmeralda Agrón, señora
I know I've no right to speak
My son is not the savage boy you see
The cape, the sneer, the slicked-back hair
Hides the child I nursed and bathed, señora

Please don't turn your eyes from me
Your son, gone to God, and mine to blame
My fated son, he too is gone
The state will see to that, I am sure, señora
The state will see to that, I am sure

MRS. YOUNG

You Spanish people, you come to this country
Nothing here changes your lives
Ungrateful immigrants, asking for pity
When all of your answers are knives
This city makes a cartoon of a crime
Capes and umbrellas, the glorification of slime
I have to face this horror, señora

MRS. KRZESINSKI

My religion asks me to pray for the murderer's soul
But I think you'd have to be Jesus on the cross
To open your heart after such a loss
Can I forgive him?
Can I forgive him?
No, I cannot

Friends become strangers
Compassion is hard to express in words
The trembling flowers they bring
Fear in the roots and the stem
What happened to me, they know could happen to them
Can I forgive him?
No, I cannot
Can I forgive him?
No

ESMERALDA

Only God can say "Forgive"
His son too received a knife
But we go on, we have to live
With this cross we call our life

MRS. YOUNG

It feels like a bomb fell
And wave after wave come the aftershocks

MRS. KRZESINSKI

You can't believe that it's true
There must be some mistake
You drift through this nightmare
From which you can't wake

Can I forgive him?
Can I forgive him?
No, I cannot

ESMERALDA

Can I forgive him?   Only God can say "Forgive"
Can I forgive him?
No, I cannot   His son too received a knife
Can I forgive him?   We go on
Can I forgive him?   We have to live
No, I cannot
Can I forgive him?
No

From *The Capeman*

SAL

It was the morning of October 6th, 1960
I was wearing my brown suit
Preparing to leave the House of D
Shook some hands, then *adios,* Brooklyn *amigos*
Maybe some of them had hopes of seeing me again
Some even said that my judge—Judge Gerald Culkin—
Wouldn't play it by the book
Maybe let us off the hook
But, whoa, I knew better

SAL AND SALVADOR

Afraid to leave the projects
To cross into another neighborhood

SAL

The *blancos* and the nigger gangs
Well, they'd kill you if they could

AUREA

Angel of Mercy, people are suffering
All over the world
Spanish children are taught on their knees to believe
Angel of Mercy, people are suffering
All over the island tonight
Mothers weep, sisters grieve

SAL

Well, I entered the courtroom
State of New York, County of New York
Just some spic
They scrubbed off the sidewalk
Guilty by my dress
Guilty in the press
"Let the Capeman burn for the murders"

Well, the Spanish boys had their day in court
And now it was time for some fuckin' law and order
"The electric chair
For the greasy pair"
Said the judge to the court reporter

SAL AND SALVADOR

Afraid to leave the projects
To cross into another neighborhood

SALVADOR

The newspapers and the TV crews
Well, they'd kill you if they could

AUREA

Angel of Mercy, people are suffering
All over the world
A Spanish boy could be killed every night of the week

SAL

But just let some white boy die
And the world goes crazy for blood—Latin blood

275

SAL AND SALVADOR

I don't lie when I speak
Well, they shackled my hands

SAL

A heavy belt around my waist to restrain me

SAL AND SALVADOR

And they shackled my legs

SAL

Hernandez, the "Umbrella Man," chained beside me
Then we rode that Black Maria
Through the streets of Spanish Harlem

SALVADOR

Calling old friends on the corners
Just to lay our prayers upon them

276

SALVADOR, SAL AND HERNANDEZ

Crying, *"Adios, hermanos, adios"*
Adios, hermanos, adios

From *The Capeman*

Jesús Es Mi Señor

FIRST CONGREGANT

¡Alabao sea Cristo!

CONGREGATION

Aleluya!
My salvation!
Aleluya!
My salvation!
Aleluya!
My salvation!
Aleluya!

FIRST CONGREGANT

He is the Prince of Peace
He walks the angry ocean
The doves of my release
Rise in His devotion

277

CONGREGATION

My soul belongs to Jesus

CONGREGATION (MEN)

Jesús es mi Señor

AUREA

I want to thank the Lord, whose mercy is a rainbow
Of comfort to my mother
I thank the governor, who heard the Lord's command
To spare the life of my brother

BERNADETTE

He is the morning sun
Who lights the desert mountain
He leads the thirsty one
Unto the silver fountain

CONGREGATION

My soul belongs to Jesus

CONGREGATION (MEN)

Jesús es mi Señor

SECOND CONGREGANT

For Eleanor Roosevelt, who spoke up for the boy
She has our gratitude and we would like to tell her

CONGREGATION

Gracias!

278

THIRD CONGREGANT

For *Doña* Fela
The mayor of San Juan

FOURTH CONGREGANT

And Governor Nelson Rockefeller

CONGREGATION

No matter where I go
No matter where I stray
No matter if I stumble
Along the way
My soul
My soul belongs to Jesus

CONGREGATION (MEN)

Jesús es mi Señor

GONZALEZ

We must remember, in the court of mighty God
No man can ever change his sentence
He is a falling angel pitched to burning hell
Till he's covered in the ashes of repentance
I tried to teach him the Devil is our shadow
And follows us wherever we go
He flew with bats and the vermin of their name
Brought everlasting shame to Puerto Rico

279

AUREA

Your heart is blacker than the suit you always wear
You who pretend to be God's disciple
He's not your own blood, so you give his life away
A hypocrite who hides behind the Bible

ESMERALDA

How can you say such things about my son?
I've been a good wife, a good wife
This marriage is done

AUREA

For three long years, my mother prayed for this to come
And wept until her eyes were empty
We made America the land we call our home
We still believe in this country

CONGREGATION

No matter where I go
No matter where I stray
No matter if I stumble
Along the way
My soul belongs to Jesus

ESMERALDA

No matter where I go
No matter where . . .

CONGREGATION (WOMEN)

My soul belongs to Jesus

CONGREGATION (MEN)

Jesús es mi Señor

LAZARUS

He is the morning sun
Who lights the desert mountain
He leads the thirsty one
Unto the silver fountain

CONGREGATION

My soul belongs to Jesus

CONGREGATION (MEN)

Jesús es mi Señor

CONGREGATION

Aleluya!
My salvation!
Aleluya!
My salvation!
Aleluya!
My salvation!
Caminando
Aleluya!
Aleluya!

From *The Capeman*

281

Sunday Afternoon

ESMERALDA

Salvador, the afternoon sunlight
Is folding around us
The dishes are done
The buildings here, tall as our mountains
Slice through the windows and cut off the sun

On such days, I find I am longing for Puerto Rico
Though I never would return 'til you are free
But when I hear the *Aguinaldo,* my heart's a little lighter
And we dance together, Aurea and me

In my life, I've been unlucky with two husbands
Gumersindo liked his rum and women friends
Then that hypocrite who beat you, and preached about repentance
Has gone, and so another Sunday ends

And tomorrow is another hardworking Monday
I'm still hoping for the raise they promised me
There's a job as operator
I would not have to wait for
If I could speak the language easily

But I tell Aurea
The *Barrio's* boundaries are our own little nation
Sometimes I hear you run upstairs
And I view my light with resignation
Keep your Bible near you
Time is an ocean of endless tears

From *The Capeman*

Time Is an Ocean

SAL

I speak to you in Jesus' name
As Jesus speaks through me
The evil we do can't be blamed
Upon our destiny
I have walked through the valley of Death Row
To the shore
I have stumbled through silvery water
To my savior, my Salvador

SALVADOR

It took me four years to learn
I was in prison, not in church
And two more to begin the book of my soul's search

SAL AND SALVADOR

Time is an ocean of endless tears

283

SALVADOR

A wild boy from the streets of *El Barrio*
The orphan from the hills of Mayagüez
And when I wrote my story
The words flew from the page
And my soul in solitary
Escaped its iron cage

Time is an ocean of endless tears

Mama, I got your letter today
The next time that you write
I'll be transferred far away
I'm leaving Green Haven's towers of stone
Where the Latin population will soon be minus one

Time is an ocean of endless tears

I know how hard it's been for you these many years
You say the *Aguinaldo*

284   Makes you dream of home

Where once we strolled the beach

At *El Malecón*

Go back, don't you worry

SAL AND SALVADOR

I am your grown-up son

SALVADOR

The politics of prison are a mirror of the street
The poor endure oppression
The police control the state
"Correctional facility"
That's what they call this place
But look around and you will see
The politics of race

SAL

A forest and a prison
Where the snow and the guards are white

SALVADOR

If you want to keep your sanity
You'll teach yourself to write
You were a child of sixteen
With a twelve-year-old mind
You came here, numb and battered
By the streets I left behind

SAL AND SALVADOR

I'll take the evil in me
And turn it into good
Though all your institutions
Never thought I could

SAL

So now I turn to say good-bye

SALVADOR

I'll keep your image in my eye

SAL AND SALVADOR

So now I turn to say good-bye

SALVADOR

I'll keep your image with me

SAL AND SALVADOR

'Til the day I die

ESMERALDA

Time is an ocean of endless tears

286

SALVADOR, ESMERALDA AND SAL

Time is an ocean of endless tears
Time is an ocean of endless tears

From   *The Capeman*

Wahzinak's First Letter

WAHZINAK

Dear Salvador Agrón
I've read your prison writings
We share a common bond
People of color must keep fighting
I live here in the desert
You need not write me back
I hope one day I'll ease your hurt
Yours truly, Wahzinak

From *The Capeman*

287

Killer Wants to Go to College

FIRST INMATE

Killer wanna go to college
Wants to get his parole
So the Department of Corrections
Can release him in the fall

Killer wanna go on TV
Wants to talk about his book
"Make my life into a movie
I got the style, I got the look"

WARDEN

This boy used to be on Death Row
Will his violence return?
Will he call out to his mother
"Mama, you can watch me burn"?

FIRST INMATE

Killer wanna go to college
Another bullshit degree
Tell the little town of New Paltz
"You ain't got nuttin' to be a-scared about wit' me"

From *The Capeman*

Virgil

VIRGIL

I've got a wife and four grown children
I can't afford their education
I been a prison guard for fourteen years
That ain't exactly a vacation

WARDEN

Since he's been here, he's followed every rule
And I've told you my position
The law says he's got the right to go to school
We abide by the court's decision

VIRGIL

I got a Winchester .243
I like that gun for deer
Upstate November, when the air is free
Smells like hunting season's here

He's the one you got to keep your eyes on
He's smart, yep, sneaky quiet
A troublemaker if I've ever seen one
Next thing it's Attica
And we got a riot

There ain't no way that punk gets his degree
And hides behind the Constitution
No way in hell that smart-ass spic goes free
Not while I'm in this institution

From *The Capeman*

SALVADOR

I write as darkness climbs these prison walls
And when I'm safe from prying eyes
I part your lips, soft as bougainvillea
I feel you in your letters

WAHZINAK

My Sal, I understand
The anger that surrounds you
But now, I take your hand
And guide it through my thighs
My dream lover, wrap your legs around me
I feel your manhood, stroke your long black hair and weary eyes

We're both alike
We're spirits of imagination
You'll love the colors of the desert, gold and rust
Puerto Rican blood blending with Indian
In a sacred flame of burning lust

290

SALVADOR AND WAHZINAK

The quarter moon stares through my window
And reads your letters on my bed
I know they open all the mail I send you
But love can't be censored

We share a history
The white man broke our nation
The braves don't know the glories of our past
The *Barrio* is just another reservation
But the day of revolution is coming fast

The desert moon is my witness
I went to pump some water from the well
I saw wild horses mating in the sunrise
I dreamed of freedom
For me and you, Sal

Oh, my darling, darling Sal

F r o m *The Capeman*

My Only Defense

S AL

I know you're trying to protect me
Searching for another truth
With your language and your poetry
From my ignorance and youth
Hey, I did not come to argue
My life never made much sense
I just wish that I could hug you
You're my only defense

I don't understand your writing
I can barely sign my name
All I ever learned was fighting
But I'm not the only one to blame
The streets were dark with danger
I had to stand up for my friends
In a land where I'm a stranger
And the hatred never ends

292

From *The Capeman*

Virgil & the Warden

VIRGIL

You playin' that spic music loud in your cell
How many times I got to warn you?

SALVADOR

I'm listening on headphones, Virgil
Why don't you just go to hell?
I'm gonna write another grievance report on you

VIRGIL

Oh, yeah, you're a famous author now
I've seen you on the tube
Got your liberal lawyers up from New York City
You're a goddamned hernia in the prison system
But me, I'm just a rube
You think the warden'll support you?
You're crazy

293

SALVADOR

I got a right to see the warden

VIRGIL

Oh, sí, you got rights

WARDEN

"I sleep with one eye open
Shadows cross my bed
I'm asking for protection
My blood is on your head"

There's the fucking contradiction
In the writing that you do
You treat your crime as fiction
When the opposite is true

Now, Sal, you better listen
The Department of Corrections is considering your parole
You got five months left in this prison
If you don't lose control

Take him back to his cell

VIRGIL

I got a Winchester .243
I like that gun for deer
Nobody's asking, but if it come down to me
I'll use that rifle right here

SALVADOR

I'm telling you straight, Virgil
If this harassment goes on
You better find another brown-skinned boy to kill
'Cause I won't wait for my parole, I'll be gone

You understand that?

VIRGIL

Oh, I understand, yeah
Shall I send for your limo, *señor*?

From *The Capeman*

Trailways Bus

LAZARUS

A passenger traveling quietly conceals himself
With a magazine and a sleepless pillow
Over the crest of the mountain
The moon begins its climb
And he wakes to find
He's in rolling farmland

The farmer sleeps against his wife
He wonders what their life must be
A Trailways bus is heading south
Into Washington, DC

A mother and child—the baby maybe two months old
Prepare themselves for sleep and feeding
The shadow of the Capitol dome
Slides across his face
And his heart is racing
With the urge to freedom

295

The father motionless as stone
A shepherd resting with his flock
The Trailways bus is turning west
Dallas via Little Rock

WAHZINAK

Oh, my darling, darling Sal
The desert moon is my witness
I've no money to come East
But I know you'll soon be here

LAZARUS

We pull into downtown Dallas
By the side of the grassy knoll
Where the leader fell, and a town was broken
Away from the feel and flow of life for so many years
He hears music playing and Spanish spoken

The border patrol outside of Tucson boarded the bus

BORDER PATROLMAN

Any aliens here, you better check with us
How 'bout you, son?
You look like you've got Spanish blood
Do you *"habla inglés"*? Am I understood?

SALVADOR

Yes, I am an alien from Mars
I come to earth from outer space
And if I traveled my whole life
You guys would still be on my case
You guys would still be on my case

LAZARUS

But he can't leave his fears behind
He recalls each fatal thrust
The screams carried by the wind
Phantom figures in the dust
Phantom figures in the dust
Phantom figures in the dust

From *The Capeman*

El Malecón

Free!
That black ribbon highway
Rolling away from me
Beyond the Spanish mission
That the sun has bleached to bone
The sky is white as marble
On the beach at *El Malecón*

El Malecón
Where all the big boats used to come
I called myself their captain
And dreamed of the day that I'd be gone

My father, Gumersindo
In the field, cutting cane
The cane rose like the ocean
And the ocean smelled of rain

El Malecón
I guide my sister's hand
My mother's watching over us
As we traced her shadow on the sand
Her hair was dark as the sea at night
Her face quiet as the moon
And we filled her skirt with the shells we liked
From the beach at *El Malecón*

The sea
The sea

From *The Capeman*

297

You Fucked Up My Life

Bara súwà yo omo yàl àwà'nà
Màmà kè'ní ir'awo-e

ANGEL SOTO

Oye, motherfuckers
Well, look who took a walk
All the way down from the jails
Of upstate New York
Well, it's Big Foot Sal, Machine Gun Sal
El Barrio's fool, and my old pal
Come back to check out the old neighborhood
You had your moment of glory
With your pearl-handled knife
Oh, what a TV story
But you fucked up my life

My mother cried in disgrace
My father cussed me out to my face
But you with your innocent eyes
You fucked up my life

BABU CHARLIE CRUZ

Do you recognize me?
I think you do
Babu Charlie Cruz
I was on trial with you
You would walk into the courtroom
Saying, "All youse are gonna burn"
As if everything evil was Puerto Rican
You know, I could have had a union job
I could have made ends meet
I didn't need to end up no ex-con
Dead-end hustling

On the street and
You had your moment of glory
With your pearl-handled knife
Oh, what a TV story
But you fucked up my life
I had a girl I was gonna marry
She left me when I was in penitentiary
Well, that's just the roll of the dice
But you, you fucked up my life

SAL

Oye, motherfuckers
Do I have to listen to this shit?
I took the weight for all of youse
And this is the thanks I get?
Stick it to the *Jibaro*
He's dumb enough to brag
He don't kiss ass in no courtroom
With the fucking American flag
Big Foot Sal, Crazy Sal
Too burned out to know better
And too stupid anyhow
There was no blood on my knife
No blood on my cape
No blood on my shoes
I was the "escape goat" for youse
You all came to gangbang
There were other guys with knives
But I'm the only murderer
When the Irish judge arrives

SALVADOR

I am an innocent man
And I paid you with my life
I am an innocent man
And I paid you with my life
I've got nothing to gain
I had done my time
And whether or not
I have committed this crime
In the eyes of the world
I am the Capeman now
For the rest of my life

HERNANDEZ

You can lie to yourself
You can lie to the press
You can lie to the cameras

HERNANDEZ AND VAMPIRES

But you cannot lie to us

HERNANDEZ

I was there at your side
The dagger in your hand

SALVADOR

I swear, by this medal of Saint Lazarus I wear
I am an innocent man

From *The Capeman*

Lazarus

When you stand on the verge of the highway to Tucson
Your shadow like a cape
Maybe your ride won't ask about prison
But your soul has no escape
And that woman on the horizon
Her joys will never be known
'Til you start your confession
In your Savior's name, Agrón

There, on the border, past mesquite and sage
Where the river glistens like knives
The denied ones carry their baggage
And dream of better lives
My hand will let them in
If you confess your sin

Chorus

Heal, healing prayer
Break a branch to cross the river over there
To deliver us salvation
With his promise, in the morning of creation

Salvador

First of all, I come with nothing
That's all a sinner receives
Even these days of freedom
Are less than a season's lease
So you followed me across the country
And shared its light on a bus
You're the stranger I wouldn't talk to
Now you're Saint Lazarus
Well, then, where is the rain you promised me

When I was a child?
Do you think I've got no memory
When my brain was monkey-wild?
I am not that fool from Mayagüez
I lived in hell for sixteen years
I'm past belief in childhood's prayers

LAZARUS

You killed and then you smiled

SALVADOR

I know remorse would be a river
In the desert of my heart
Whose loss is God, the giver
But my tears won't start
The State of New York imprisoned me
The State of New York will set me free
I break this chain, its pain and its memory

MRS. KRZESINSKI

Sixteen years and still I weep
And wish that I had died that day
I've grown weary in my step
But I cannot turn away

Every year, I light a candle
On the day that he was born
For the life he never tasted
For his children never come
I've grown weary, I've grown old
But I'll never be at rest
'Til the murder that you did
Is paid for
With the last drop of blood

Go live in an empty room
And study the wallpaper
No wife, no child, in that home
Let your solitude frighten your neighbor
And write in your book
With your cunning prisoner's hand
How arrogant you were
How ordinary as the sand
Then burrow down, deep as the mole
Blind 'til your release
But neither pardon nor parole
Will ever bring you peace

CHORUS

Heal, healing prayer
Scent of desert flowers in the air
To deliver us salvation
With His promise, in the morning of creation
Reza, reza por nuestra salvación
Reza, reza por nuestra salvación

303

From *The Capeman*

Wahzinak's Last Letter

WAHZINAK

Oh, my darling Sal
They made me bury your letters
I went out before the morning light
Accompanied by two elders
And every word you wrote me with your loving hand
Is buried now forever, in the blowing desert sand

From *The Capeman*

304

All across the city, the party has begun
From Brownsville, in Brooklyn
Hunts Point in the Bronx
El Barrio in Harlem
To the Lower East Side
It's a day of celebration
And Latin pride

Puerto Rican Day parade
Hey, *Boricua*
Lay-lo, lai, lo-lay

Puerto Rican Day parade
Hey, *Boricua*
Lay-lo, lai, lo-lay

Piraguas, banderas, coquíto, cerveza fría

Puerto Rican Day parade
Hey, *Boricua*
Lay-lo, lai, lo-lay

Puerto Rican Day parade
Hey, *Boricua*
Lay-lo, lai, lo-lay

Porqué soy Puertorriqueño

Boricua, lay-lo, lai

En borinquen yo nací

Boricua, lay-lo, lai

Oye, soy hermano del coquí

Boricua, lay-lo, lai

Borinquen, cómo te quiero

Boricua, lay-lo, lai

From *The Capeman*

El Coquí (Reprise)

CHILDREN (OFFSTAGE)

El coquí, el coquí a mi me encanta
Es tan lindo el cantar del coquí
Por las noches al ir a acostarme
Me adormece cantando asi
Coquí, coquí, coquí, quí, quí, quí!
Coquí, coquí, coquí, quí, quí, quí!

SALVADOR

Hey, Yolanda, I'm almost there
I'm calling from a pay phone
On the corner, somewhere
Tell Carlos I'll be by for my things
Don't tell my mother I'm home yet

From *The Capeman*

307

HERNANDEZ

You know it takes a strong man to survive

SALVADOR

Tony, Tony, is that you? Man, I thought you were dead

HERNANDEZ

No, man, just living in the Bronx

SALVADOR

Well, same thing, that's what I said

HERNANDEZ

I know your parole board don't want us to meet each other
That's why I'm not in the light
But I see you now, my Death Row brother
And it looks like you made it alright

SALVADOR

I'm going to see Carlos and Yolanda
Come on and walk by my side

HERNANDEZ

I don't like to see nobody, only you

SALVADOR

Well, it ain't like we gotta hide
So, how you been doing?

HERNANDEZ

Doing the best I can
I got a job at Beekman Downtown Hospital
Working as a cleaning man
But there's one stain that don't fade
You know what I'm talking about, Sal?

SALVADOR

Yeah

HERNANDEZ

It's the first time you seen the parade?

SALVADOR

Yes, it's nice
I'll be glad to see my mother

309

HERNANDEZ

My father passed away

SALVADOR

Oh, I'm sorry

But I've got a little daughter
It balances, so I guess it's okay
Give your moms my love
When I look up at the sky above
It's like an old umbrella with holes
I'm glad I seen you
Write a big best seller
And may God accept our souls

From *The Capeman*

310

CARLOS

Hey, *amigo!* How you feeling? You're looking good

SALVADOR

I feel alright
But it's strange, you know
Like I'm a ghost wandering in the neighborhood

CARLOS

The mind, the mind plays games with you
When you first breathe freedom's air
I did my time, and when my stretch was through
Thank God, Yolanda was there

SALVADOR

Señor Carlos Apache

CARLOS

Señor Salvador Agrón

SALVADOR

See how the mirror's changed our faces?
My father's eyes are now my own

CARLOS

The parade is almost over
In my office I've kept your papers safe and sound
The guy who brought them took no money
He just shook my hand and turned around

CHORUS

Mi libertad
Mi libertad, llego

SALVADOR

I wrote these pages not with ink, but blood

CARLOS

That's the kind of stuff that sells

SALVADOR

Yes, but that's not why I did it, Carlos

CARLOS

Boricua, you got to eat like everybody else

SALVADOR

Do you ever see the guys we knew?

CARLOS

Oh, yeah, they come down when they need a dime to score

SALVADOR

The Capeman, I'll never shake that name

CARLOS

No one remembers anymore

YOLANDA

Sal, this is Carlito
Carlito, your uncle Sal

SALVADOR

Oh, my gosh, he's so big. How are you?

CARLITO

Are you the Capeman?

SALVADOR

I used to be your father's pal

YOLANDA

You always will be, Salvador   313

SALVADOR

You still feel the same way about me, Carlos?
Or in your mind, was I the only one?

CARLOS

But Sal, it was dark, so long ago, you and Tony . . .

YOLANDA

My God, what's done is done

M.C.

Who will buy these raffle tickets
I have in my hand?
The proceeds earmarked for the San Juan Bautista chapel
Win a trip to our Puerto Rican homeland
Leave your worries and your kids in the Big Apple
We know the legend of the coquí
The frog who blessed our island with his song
We may live in New York City (*Boricua!*)
But it's Puerto Rico where our hearts belong

Mi libertad
Mi libertad, llego
Mi libertad
Mi libertad, llego

From *The Capeman*

314

SALVADOR

Mama, please forgive me all the pain
If I could cleanse these hands, maybe then
I could start my life again

ESMERALDA

You have come to the end of the Santa Cruz Road

SALVADOR

There is something I must tell you
I and I alone
Never the santero
I and I alone
Must bear the blame
For the madness that was done
For the shame that I have brought upon the name Agrón
I and I alone

315

When the shells were thrown
When the cape was worn
When the summer night was torn
By the dagger of the moon
It was I and I alone

ESMERALDA

Salvador, I dreamed of this moment
The sound of your footsteps
Your face in the light
Let me kiss your hands, no more talk about madness
I've been cooking since morning
I wanted your first meal at home to be right

SALVADOR

This is my book, I've written my life story
It begins that starlit night up on the hill
Then all the things I did, for which I am sorry

ESMERALDA

It is repentance that makes good from evil

From *The Capeman*

316

Esmeralda's Dream

I was sitting in an outer room in heaven
Wearing the housedress that I always wore
And I was watching these two angels from a distance
Say, from where you're sitting now to the corner store
There was a pulpit and a small chair in the office
Made of wood without comparison on Earth
The doors were all of marble, but transparent
They were writing in a book your date of birth

Do you remember the asilo's first communion?
All the children with their candles dressed in white
And once in prison, you asked me for a ribbon
To mark the pages that you wrote each night

Do you remember when we went to the santero
And he said that you would suffer
He was right

SAL

I believe I'm in the power of Saint Lazarus
Don't tear apart this satin summer night

Whoa
Whoa
Whoa

ESMERALDA

The angels both were male and softly spoken
Their hair was lightened by the sea and sun
They carried a chain, the chain was broken
Then they laid it at my feet and they were gone

Whoa

Whoa

Whoa

From *The Capeman*

1999–2008

You're the One
  That's Where I Belong
  Darling Lorraine
  Old
  You're the One
  The Teacher
  Look at That
  Señorita With a Necklace of Tears
  Love
  Pigs, Sheep and Wolves
  Hurricane Eye
  Quiet

Surprise
  How Can You Live in the Northeast?
  Everything About It Is a Love Song
  Outrageous
  Sure Don't Feel Like Love
  Wartime Prayers
  Beautiful
  I Don't Believe
  Another Galaxy
  Once Upon a Time There Was an Ocean
  That's Me
  Father and Daughter

Somewhere in a burst of glory
Sound becomes a song
I'm bound to tell a story
That's where I belong

When I see you smiling
When I hear you singing
Lavender and roses
Every ending a beginning
The way you turn
And catch me with your eye
Ay ay ay
That's where I belong

When I see you smiling
When I hear you singing
Lavender and roses
Every ending a beginning
That's the way it is
I don't know why
Ay ay ay
But that's where I belong

A spiny little island man
Plays a jingling banjo
He's walking down a dirt road
Carrying his radio
To a river where the water meets the sky
Ay ay ay
That's where I belong

From the album *You're the One*

322

The first time I saw her
I couldn't be sure
But the sin of impatience
Said, "She's just what you're looking for"
So I walked right up to her
And with the part of me that talks
I introduced myself as Frank
From New York, New York
She's so hot
She's so cool
I'm not
I'm just a fool in love with darling Lorraine

All my life I've been a wanderer
Not really, I mostly lived near my parents' home
Anyway, Lorraine and I got married
And the usual marriage stuff
Then one day she says to me
From out of the blue
She says, "Frank, I've had enough
Romance is a heartbreaker
I'm not meant to be a homemaker
And I'm tired of being darling Lorraine"

What—you don't love me anymore?
What—you're walking out the door?
What—you don't like the way I chew?
Hey, let me tell you
You're not the woman that I wed
You say you're depressed but you're not
You just like to stay in bed
I don't need you, darling Lorraine
Darling Lorraine

323

Lorraine
I long for your love

Financially speaking
I guess I'm a washout
Everybody's buy and sell
And sell and buy
And that's what the whole thing's all about

If it had not been for Lorraine
I'd have left here long ago
I should have been a musician
I love the piano
She's so light
She's so free
I'm tight, well, that's me
But I feel so good
With darling Lorraine

On Christmas morning, Frank awakes
To find Lorraine has made a stack of pancakes
They watch the television, husband and wife
All afternoon, *It's a Wonderful Life*

What—you don't love me anymore?
What—you're walking out the door?
What—you don't like the way I chew?
Hey, let me tell you
You're not the woman that I wed
Gimme my robe, I'm going back to bed
I'm sick to death of you, Lorraine

Darling Lorraine
Lorraine
Her hands like wood
The doctor was smiling
But the news wasn't good

Darling Lorraine
Please don't leave me yet
I know you're in pain
Pain you can't forget
Your breathing is like an echo of our love
Maybe I'll go down to the corner store
And buy us something sweet
Here's an extra blanket, honey
To wrap around your feet
All the trees were washed with April rain
And the moon in the meadow
Took darling Lorraine

From the album *You're the One*

Old

The first time I heard "Peggy Sue"
I was twelve years old
Russians up in rocket ships
And the war was cold
Now many wars have come and gone
Genocide still goes on
Buddy Holly still goes on
But his catalog was sold

First time I smoked
Guess what? Paranoid.
First time I heard "Satisfaction"
I was young and unemployed
Down the decades every year
Summer leaves and my birthday's here
And all my friends stand up and cheer
And say, "Man, you're old"
Getting old
Old
You're getting old

We celebrate the birth of Jesus on Christmas Day
And Buddha found nirvana along the lotus way
About 1,500 years ago the messenger Mohammed spoke
And his wisdom like a river flowed
Through hills of gold
Wisdom is old
The Koran is old
The Bible is old
Greatest story ever told

Disagreements?
Work 'em out

The human race has walked the earth for 2.7 million
And we estimate the universe about 13–14 billion
When all these numbers tumble into your imagination
Consider that the Lord was there before creation
God is old
We're not old
God is old
He made the mold

Take your clothes off
Adam and Eve

From the album *You're the One*

May twelve angels guard you
While you sleep
Maybe that's a waste of angels, I don't know
I'd do anything to keep you safe
From the danger that surrounds us

Little by little
Bit by bit
Little bit by little bit
Now you got it, that's it
What're you thinking
Things'll go sour?
Take its temperature every hour
Nervous when you own it
Nervous when it's gone
What do you think has been going on
For so long?

You are the air
Inside my chest
You're the one
You broke my heart
You made me cry
You're the one
You broke my heart
You made me cry
You're the one
You broke my heart
You made me cry
You're the one

But when I hear it from the other side
It's a completely different song
And I'm the one who made you cry
And I'm the one who's wrong
And in my dream, you spoke to me
And you said, you said

You're the one
You broke my heart
You made me cry
You're the one
You broke my heart
You made me cry
You're the one
You broke my heart
You made me cry
You're the one

Nature gives us changing shapes
Clouds and waves and flame
But human expectation
Is that love remains the same
And when it doesn't
We point our fingers
And blame, blame, blame

You're the one
You broke my heart
You made me cry
And I'm the one
I broke your heart
I made you cry
And you're the one
You broke my heart
You made me cry
And we're the ones

329

From the album *You're the One*

The Teacher

There once was a teacher of great renown
Whose words were like tablets of stone
"Because it's easier to learn than unlearn
Because we've passed the point of no return
Gather your goods and follow me
Or you will surely die"

I was only a child of the city
My parents were children of immigrant stock
So we followed as followers go
Over the mountain with a napkin of snow
And ate the berries and roots
That grow along the timberline

Deeper and deeper the dreamer of love
Sleeps on a quilt of stars

It's cold
Sometimes you can't catch your breath
It's cold

Time and abundance thickened his step
So the teacher divided in two
One half ate the forests and the fields
The other half sucked all the moisture from the clouds
And we, we were amazed at the power of his appetite

Deeper and deeper the dreamer of love
Sleeps on a quilt of stars

Sometimes we don't know who we are
Sometimes force overpowers us and we cry
My teacher, carry me home
Carry me home, my teacher
Carry me home
Carry me home, my teacher
Carry me home
Carry me home, my teacher
Carry me home

From the album *You're the One*

Look at that
Look at this
Drop a stone in the abyss
Then walk away and know that anything can happen
Just like that
Just like this

Look at that
Look at this
Gimme a hug, gimme a kiss
Hey, hey, and off to school we go
You might learn something
Yeah, you never know
I love you so

Look at that
Look at this
Lovers merge and make a wish
They close their eyes and now their dreams are legal
And on the horizon, the eagle flies
Through clouds of fire
Swoop and glide
You can't believe it
You can't decide

333

Ask somebody to love you
Takes a lot of nerve
Ask somebody to love you
You got a lot of nerve
Ask somebody to love you
Takes a lot of nerve
Ask somebody to love you
Ma ma ma ma
Ma ma ma ma
Da da da da

Da da da da
La la la la
La la la la
Oom bop a doom

Look at that
Look at this
This is near enough to bliss
Then over the top we go and down
Down to the bottom
If you're looking for worries
You got 'em

Ask somebody to love you
You got a lot of nerve
Ask somebody to love you
Takes a lot of nerve
Tih tih tih tih
Tih tih tih tih
Guh guh guh guh
Guh guh guh guh
Lih lih lih lih
Lih lih lih lih
Oom bop a doom

Come awake, come alive
Common sense, we survive
Then hey, hey, down the road we go
You might learn something
Yeah, you never know
But anyway, you've got to go

From the album *You're the One*

I have a wisdom tooth
Inside my crowded face
I have a friend who is a born-again
Found his Savior's grace
I was born before my father
And my children before me
And we are born and born again
Like the waves of the sea
That's the way it's always been
And that's how I want it to be
That's the way it's always been
And that's how I want it to be

Nothing but good news
There is a frog in South America
Whose venom is a cure
For all the suffering
That mankind must endure
More powerful than morphine
And soothing as the rain
A frog in South America
Has the antidote for pain
That's the way it's always been
And that's the way I like it

Some people never say no
Some people never complain
Some folks have no idea
And others will never explain
That's the way it's always been
That's the way I like it
And that's how I want it to be
That's the way it's always been
That's the way I like it
And that's how I want it to be

335

If I could play all the memories
In the neck of my guitar
I would write a song called
"Señorita with a Necklace of Tears"
And every tear a sin I'd committed
Oh these many years
That's who I was
That's the way it's always been

Some people always want more
Some people are what they lack
Some folks open a door
Walk away and never look back
And I don't want to be a judge
And I don't want to be a jury
I know who I am
Lord knows who I will be
That's the way it's always been
That's the way I like it
And that's how I want it to be
That's the way it's always been
And that's the way I like it
And that's how I want it to be

From the album *You're the One*

Love

Cool me
Cool my fever high
Hold me when I cry
I need it so much
Makes you want to get down and crawl like a beggar
For its touch
And all the while, it's free as air
Like plants, the medicine is everywhere

Love
Love
Love

We crave it so badly
Makes you want to laugh out loud when you receive it
And gobble it like candy

We think it's easy
Sometimes it's easy
But it's not easy
You're going to break down and cry
We're not important
We should be grateful
And if you're wondering why, why

Love
Love
Love

The price that we pay
When evil walks the planet
And love is crushed like clay
The master races, the chosen peoples
The burning temples, the weeping cathedrals

33₇

From the album *You're the One*

Big and fat
Pig's supposed to look like that
Barnyard thug
Sleeps on straw and he calls it a rug
Yeah, that's a rug, okay
He's walking down the street
And nobody's gonna argue with him
He's a half a ton of pig meat

Up in the hills above the farm
Lives a pack of wolves
Never did no harm
Sleep all day
Hunt till four
Maybe catch a couple of rodents
You know, carnivore

Sheep in the meadow
Nibbling on some clover
One of those sheep wanders over
Sits by a rock
Separated from the flock
He's just sitting by a rock

Where'd he go?
I don't know
Well, he was here a minute ago
I don't know
Sheep's dead
Got a gash as big as a wolf's head
Oh, God

338

Big and fat
Pig's supposed to look like that
Wallowing in lanolin
He's rubbing it into his pigskin
Police are going crazy
Say, let's get him
Let's get that wolf
Let's get him
Let's get that wolf
Let's get him
Let's kill him, let's get him
Let's kill him

Court-appointed lawyer wasn't very bright
Oh, maybe he was bright
Maybe it was just a late night
Yeah, it was just a late night
And he files some feeble appeal
And the governor says, "Forget it
It's a done deal
It's election, I don't care, election
Let's give that wolf a lethal injection"
Let's get him, yeah, let's get that wolf,
Let's kill him, let's get him
Let's kill him, let's get him, kill him
Let's get him and kill him

339

Whew, slow
Here come the media
With their camera
Asking everybody's opinion
About pigs, sheep and wolves

Big and fat
Pig's supposed to laugh like that
"This is hilarious
What a great time
I'm the pig who committed
The perfect crime"

All around the world
France and Scandinavia
Candlelight vigils
Protesting this behavior
It's animal behavior
Animal behavior
It's pigs, sheep and wolves
Pigs, sheep and wolves
Pigs, sheep and wolves
It's animal behavior
It's pigs, sheep and wolves

From the album *You're the One*

Tell us all a story
About how it used to be
Make it up and then write it down
Just like history
About Goldilocks and the three bears
Nature in the crosshairs
And how we all ascended
From the deep green sea
When it's not too hot
Not too cold
Not too meek
Not too bold
Where it's just right and you have sunlight
Then we're home
Finally home
Home in the land of the homeless
Finally home

Oh, what are we going to do?
I never did a thing to you
Time peaceful as a hurricane eye
Peaceful as a hurricane eye

A history of whispers
A shadow of a horse
Faces painted black in sorrow and remorse
White cloud, black crow
Crucifix and arrow
The oldest silence speaks the loudest
Under the deep green sea

When speech becomes a crime
Silence leads the spirit
Over the bridge of time

Over the bridge of time
I'm walking with my family
And the road begins to climb
And then it's, oh, Lord, how we gonna pray
With crazy angel voices
All night
Until it's a new day
Peaceful as a hurricane
Peaceful as a hurricane
Peaceful as a hurricane eye
Peaceful as a hurricane
Peaceful as a hurricane
Peaceful as a hurricane eye
Peaceful as a hurricane eye

You want to be leader?
You want to change the game?
Turn your back on money
Walk away from fame
You want to be a missionary?
You got that missionary zeal?
Let a stranger change your life
How's that make you feel?
You want to be a writer
But you don't know how or when
Find a quiet place
Use a humble pen

You want to talk, talk, talk about it
All night, squawk about
The ocean and the atmosphere
Well, I've been away for a long time
And it looks like a mess around here
And I'll be away for a long time
So here's how the story goes
There was an old woman
Who lived in a shoe
She was baking a cinnamon pie
She fell asleep in a washing machine
Woke up in a hurricane eye

From the album *You're the One*

343

Quiet

I am heading for a time of quiet
When my restlessness is past
And I can lie down on my blanket
And release my fists at last

I am heading for a time of solitude
Of peace without illusions
When the perfect circle marries
All beginnings and conclusions

And when they say
That you're not good enough
Well, the answer is
You're not
But who are they
Or what is it
That eats at what you've got?
With the hunger of ambition
For the change inside the purse
They are handcuffs on the soul, my friends
Handcuffs on the soul
And worse

And I am heading for a place of quiet
Where the sage and sweet grass grow
By a lake of sacred water
From the mountain's melted snow

From the album *You're the One*

PAUL SIMON

SURPRISE

How Can You Live in the Northeast?

We heard the fireworks
Rushed out to watch the sky
Happy-go-lucky, Fourth of July

How can you live in the Northeast?
How can you live in the South?
How can you build on the banks of a river when the floodwater pours
    from the mouth?
How can you be a Christian?
How can you be a Jew?
How can you be a Muslim, a Buddhist, a Hindu?
How can you?

Weak as the winter sun, we enter life on earth
Names and religion come just after date of birth
Then everybody gets a tongue to speak
And everyone hears an inner voice
A day at the end of the week
To wonder and rejoice
If the answer is infinite light, why do we sleep in the dark?

How can you live in the Northeast?
How can live in the South?
How can you build on the banks of a river when the floodwater pours
    from the mouth?
How can you tattoo your body?
Why do you cover your head?
How can you eat from a rice bowl? The holy man only breaks bread

We watched the fireworks 'til they were fireflies
Followed a path of stars
Over the endless skies

How can you live in the Northeast?
How can you live in the South?
How can you build on the banks of a river when the floodwater pours
    from the mouth?

I've been given all I wanted
Only three generations off the boat
I have harvested and I have planted
I am wearing my father's old coat

From the album *Surprise*

348

Locked in a struggle for the right combination—
Of words in a melody line
I took a walk along the riverbank of my imagination
Golden clouds were shuffling the sunshine

But if I ever get back to the twentieth century
Guess I'll have to pay off some debts
Open the book of my vanishing memory
With its catalog of regrets
Stand up for the deeds I did, and those I didn't do
Sit down, shut up, think about God
And wait for the hour of my rescue

We don't mean to mess things up, but mess them up we do
And then it's "Oh, I'm sorry"
Here's a smiling photograph of love when it was new
At a birthday party
Make a wish and close your eyes
Surprise, surprise, surprise

Early December, and brown as a sparrow
Frost creeping over the pond
I shoot a thought into the future, and it flies like an arrow
Through my lifetime, and beyond

If I ever come back as a tree, or a crow
Or even the windblown dust
Find me on the ancient road
In the song when the wires are hushed
Hurry on and remember me, as I'll remember you
Far above the golden clouds, the darkness vibrates
The earth is blue

And everything about it is a love song
Everything about it
Everything about it is a love song
Everything about it
Everything about it is a love song

From the album *Surprise*

350

Outrageous

It's outrageous to line your pockets off the misery of the poor
Outrageous, the crimes some human beings must endure
It's a blessing to wash your face in the summer solstice rain
It's outrageous a man like me stand here and complain

But I'm tired
Nine hundred sit-ups a day
I'm painting my hair the color of mud—mud, okay?
I'm tired, tired
Anybody care what I say? No!
I'm painting my hair the color of mud

Who's gonna love you when your looks are gone?
Tell me, who's gonna love you when your looks are gone?
Aw, who's gonna love you when your looks are gone?
Who's gonna love you when your looks are gone?

It's outrageous, the food they try to serve in a public school
Outrageous, the way they talk to you like you're some kind of clinical
fool
It's a blessing to rest my head in the circle of your love
It's outrageous I can't stop thinking 'bout the things I'm thinking of

And I'm tired
Nine hundred sit-ups a day
I'm painting my hair the color of mud—mud, okay?
I'm tired, tired, anybody care what I say? No!
Painting my hair the color of mud

Who's gonna love you when your looks are gone?
Tell me, who's gonna love you when your looks are gone?
Tell me, who's gonna love you when your looks are gone?

Who's gonna love you when your looks are gone?
Tell me, who's gonna love you when your looks are gone?

God will
Like He waters the flowers on your windowsill
Take me
I'm an ordinary player in the key of C
And my will
Was broken by my pride and my vanity

Who's gonna love you when your looks are gone?
God will
Like He waters the flowers on your windowsill
Who's gonna love you when your looks are gone?

From the album *Surprise*

Sure Don't Feel Like Love

I registered to vote today
Felt like a fool
Had to do it anyway
Down at the high school
Thing about the second line
You know, "Felt like a fool"?
People say it all the time
Even when it's true
So, who's that conscience sticking on the sole of my shoe?
Who's that conscience sticking on the sole of my shoe?
'Cause it sure don't feel like love

A teardrop consists of electrolytes and salt
The chemistry of crying is
Not concerned with blame or fault
So, who's that conscience sticking on the sole of my shoe?
Who's that conscience sticking on the sole of my shoe?
'Cause it sure don't feel like love

How does it feel? Feels like a threat
A voice in your head that you'd rather forget
No joke, no joke
You get sick from that unspoken
Sure don't feel like love
No joke, no joke
Some chicken and a corn muffin
Well, that feels more like love

Yay! Boo!
Yay! Boo!

353

Wrong again
Wrong again
Maybe I'm wrong again
Wrong again
Maybe I'm wrong again
Wrong again
I could be wrong again

I remember once in August 1993
I was wrong, and I could be wrong again
I remember one of my best friends turned enemy
So, I was wrong, and I could be wrong again
I remember once in a load-out, down in Birmingham
Yeah, but that didn't feel like love
Sure don't feel like, sure don't feel like, sure don't feel like love
Sure don't feel like, sure don't feel like, sure don't feel like love
It sure
Don't feel
Like love

From the album *Surprise*

354

Prayers offered in times of peace
Are silent conversations
Appeals for love, or love's release
In private invocations
But all that is changed now
Gone like a memory from the day before the fires
People hungry for the voice of God
Hear lunatics and liars

Wartime prayers
Wartime prayers
In every language spoken
For every family scattered and broken

Because you cannot walk with the holy if you're just a halfway
    decent man
I don't pretend that I'm a mastermind with a genius marketing plan
I'm trying to tap into some wisdom
Even a little drop will do
I want to rid my heart of envy
And cleanse my soul of rage before I'm through

355

Times are hard, it's a hard time
But everybody knows
All about hard times, the thing is
What are you gonna do?
Well, you cry and try to muscle through
And try to rearrange your stuff
But when the wounds are deep enough
And it's all that we can bear
We wrap ourselves in prayer

Because you cannot walk with the holy if you're just a halfway decent
man
I don't pretend that I'm a mastermind with a genius marketing plan
I'm trying to tap into some wisdom
Even a little drop will do
I want to rid my heart of envy
And cleanse my soul of rage before I'm through

A mother murmurs in twilight sleep
And draws her babies closer
With hush-a-byes for sleepy eyes
And kisses on the shoulder
To drive away despair
She says a wartime prayer

From the album *Surprise*

356

Beautiful

Snowman sittin' in the sun
Doesn't have time to waste
He had a little bit too much fun
Now his head's erased
Back in the house, family of three
Two doin' the laundry
And one in the nursery

We brought a brand-new baby back from Bangladesh
Thought we'd name her Emily
She's beautiful
Beautiful

Yes, sir, head's erased
Brain's a bowl of jelly
Hasn't hurt his sense of taste
Judging from his belly
But back in the house, family of four now
Two doin' the laundry
And two on the kitchen floor

We brought a brand-new baby back from mainland China
Sailed across the China Sea
She's beautiful
Beautiful

Go-kart sittin' in the shade
You don't need a ticket to ride
It's summertime, summertime
Slip down a waterslide
Little kid dancin' in the grass
Legs like rubber band
It's summertime, summertime
There's a line at the candy stand
You better keep an eye on them children, eye on them children in
    the pool
You better keep an eye on them children, eye on them children in
    the pool

We brought a brand-new baby back from Kosovo
That was nearly seven years ago
He cried all night, could not sleep
His eyes were bright, dark and deep
Beautiful
Beautiful

From the album *Surprise*

I Don't Believe

Acts of kindness
Like breadcrumbs in a fairy-tale forest
Lead us past dangers
As light melts the darkness
But I don't believe, and I'm not consoled
I lean closer to the fire, but I'm cold

The earth was born in a storm
The waters receded, the mountains were formed
The universe loves a drama, you know
And, ladies and gentlemen, this is the show

I got a call from my broker
The broker informed me I'm broke
I was dealing my last hand of poker
My cards were useless as smoke

Oh, guardian angel
Don't taunt me like this
On a clear summer evening
As soft as a kiss

My children are laughing, not a whisper of care
My love is brushing her long chestnut hair
I don't believe a heart can be filled to the brim
Then vanish like mist
As though life were a whim

Maybe the heart is part of the mist
And that's all that there is or could ever exist
Maybe and maybe and maybe some more
Maybe's the exit that I'm looking for

I got a call from my broker
The broker said he was mistaken
Maybe some virus or brokerage joke
And he hopes that my faith isn't shaken

Acts of kindness
Like rain in a drought
Release the spirit with a whoop and a shout
I don't believe we were born to be sheep in a flock
To pantomime prayers with the hands of a clock

From the album *Surprise*

Another Galaxy

On the morning of her wedding day
When no one was awake
She drove across the border
Leaving all the yellow roses on her wedding cake
Her mother's tears, her breakfast order
She's gone, gone, gone

There is a moment, a chip in time
When leaving home is the lesser crime
When your eyes are blind with tears, but your heart can see
Another life, another galaxy

That night, her dreams are storm-tossed as a willow
She hears the clouds
She sees the eye of a hurricane
As it sweeps across her island pillow
But she's gone, gone, gone

There is a moment, a chip in time
When leaving home is the lesser crime
When your eyes are blind with tears, but your heart can see
Another life, another galaxy

From the album *Surprise*

Once upon a time, there was an ocean
But now it's a mountain range
Something unstoppable set into motion
Nothing is different, but everything's changed

It's a dead-end job, and you get tired of sittin'
It's like a nicotine habit
You're always thinkin' about quittin'
And I think about quittin' every day of the week
When I look out my window, it's brown and it's bleak

Outta here
How'm I gonna get outta here?
I'm thinking outta here
When am I gonna get outta here?

And when will I cash in my lottery ticket
And bury my past with my burdens and strife?
I want to shake every limb in the Garden of Eden
And make every lover the love of my life

I figure that once upon a time, I was an ocean
But now I'm a mountain range
Something unstoppable set into motion
Nothing is different, but everything's changed

Found a room in the heart of the city, down by the bridge
Hot plate and TV and beer in the fridge
But I'm easy, I'm open—that's my gift
I can flow with the traffic, I can drift with the drift

Home again?
Naw, never going home again
Think about home again?
I never think about home

But then comes a letter from home
The handwriting's fragile and strange
Something unstoppable set into motion
Nothing is different, but everything's changed

The light through the stained glass was cobalt and red
And the frayed cuffs and collars
Were mended by haloes of golden thread
The choir sang, "Once Upon a Time There Was an Ocean"
And all the old hymns and family names
Came fluttering down as leaves of emotion
As nothing is different, but everything's changed

From the album *Surprise*

363

Well, I'll just skip the boring parts
Chapters one, two, three
And get to the place
Where you can read my face and my biography
Here I am, I'm eleven months old
Dangling from my daddy's knee
There I go, it's my graduation
I'm picking up a bogus degree
That's me
Early me
That's me

Well, I never cared much for the money
And money never cared for me
I was more like a landlocked sailor
Searching for the emerald sea
Just searching for the emerald sea, boys
Searching for the sea

Oh, my God
First love opens like a flower
A black bear running through the forest light
Holds me in her sight and her power
But tricky skies, your eyes are true
The future is beauty and sorrow
Still, I wish that we could run away and live the life we used to
If just for tonight and tomorrow

I am walking up the face of the mountain
Counting every step I climb
Remembering the names of the constellations
Forgotten is a long, long time
That's me
I'm in the valley of twilight
Now I'm on the continental shelf
That's me—
I'm answering a question
I am asking of myself

That's me
That's me

From the album *Surprise*

Father and Daughter

If you leap awake in the mirror of a bad dream
And for a fraction of a second, you can't remember where you are
Just open your window and follow your memory upstream
To the meadow in the mountain where we counted every falling star

I believe the light that shines on you will shine on you forever
And though I can't guarantee there's nothing scary hiding under
   your bed
I'm gonna stand guard like a postcard of a golden retriever
And never leave 'til I leave you with a sweet dream in your head

I'm gonna watch you shine
Gonna watch you grow
Gonna paint a sign
So you'll always know
As long as one and one is two
There could never be a father
Who loved his daughter more than I love you

Trust your intuition
It's just like goin' fishin'
You cast your line and hope you get a bite
But you don't need to waste your time
Worryin' about the marketplace
Try to help the human race
Struggling to survive its harshest night

I'm gonna watch you shine
Gonna watch you grow
Gonna paint a sign
So you'll always know
As long as one and one is two
There could never be a father
Who loved his daughter more than I love you

From the album *Surprise*

2009-2011

PAUL SIMON
So Beautiful or So What

Getting Ready for Christmas Day

From early in November to the last week of December
I got money matters weighing me down
Oh, the music may be merry, but it's only temporary
I know Santa Claus is coming to town

In the days I work my day job, in the nights I work my night
But it all comes down to working man's pay
Getting ready, I'm getting ready, ready for Christmas Day

R EVEREND GATES:

Getting ready for Christmas Day
And let me tell you, namely, the undertaker, he's getting ready for
    your body
Not only that, the jailer, he's getting ready for you
Christmas Day. Hmm? And not only the jailer, but the lawyer, the
    police force
Now getting ready for Christmas Day, and I want you to bear it in
    mind

I got a nephew in Iraq, it's his third time back
But it's ending up the way it began
With the luck of a beginner he'll be eating turkey dinner
On some mountaintop in Pakistan

Getting ready, oh, we're getting ready
For the power and the glory and the story of the
Christmas Day

R EVEREND GATES:

Getting ready for Christmas Day
Done made it up in your mind that I'm going, New York,
    Philadelphia, Chicago
I'm going, on a trip, getting ready for Christmas Day

369

But when Christmas come, nobody knows where you'll be
You might ask me
I may be layin' in some lonesome grave, getting ready for Christmas
	Day

Getting ready, oh, we're getting ready
For the power and the glory and the story of the
Christmas Day
Yes, we're getting ready

REVEREND GATES:

Getting ready, ready for your prayers
"I'm going and see my relatives in a distant land"
Getting ready, getting ready for Christmas Day

If I could tell my mom and dad that the things we never had
Never mattered, we were always okay
Getting ready, oh, ready, ready for Christmas Day
Ready, getting ready
For the power and the glory and the story of the
Christmas Day

From the album *So Beautiful or So What*

After I died, and the makeup had dried
I went back to my place
No moon that night, but a heavenly light
Shone on my face
Still I thought it was odd there was no sign of God
Just to usher me in
Then a voice from above, sugarcoated with love
Said, "Let us begin"

You got to fill out a form first
And then you wait in the line
You got to fill out a form first
And then you wait in the line

Okay, new kid in school, got to follow the rule
You got to learn the routine
Whoa! There's a girl over there, with the sunshiny hair
Like a homecoming queen
I said, "Hey, what'cha say, it's a glorious day
By the way, how long you been dead?"
Maybe you, maybe me, maybe baby makes three
But she just shook her head

You got to fill out a form first
And then you wait in the line
You got to fill out a form first
And then you wait in the line
Buddha and Moses and all the noses
From narrow to flat
Had to stand in the line just to glimpse the divine
What'cha think about that?
Well, it seems like our fate to suffer and wait
For the knowledge we seek
It's all His design, no one cuts in the line
No one here likes a sneak

You got to fill out a form first
And then you wait in the line
You got to fill out a form first
And then you wait in the line

After you climb up the ladder of time
The Lord God is near
Face-to-face in the vastness of space
Your words disappear
And you feel like you're swimming in an ocean of love
And the current is strong
But all that remains when you try to explain
Is a fragment of song

Lord, is it Be Bop a Lula? Or Ooh Papa Doo?
Lord, Be Bop a Lula? Or Ooh Papa Doo?
Be Bop a Lula

From the album *So Beautiful or So What*

Dazzling Blue

Truth or lie, the silence is revealing
An empty sky, a hidden mound of stone
But the CAT scan's eye sees what the heart's concealing
Nowadays, when everything is known

Maybe love's an accident, or destiny is true
But you and I were born beneath a star of dazzling blue
Dazzling blue

Miles apart, though the miles can't measure distance
Worlds apart on a rainy afternoon
But the road gets dirty and it offers no resistance
So turn your amp up and play your lonesome tune

Maybe love's an accident, or destiny is true
But you and I were born beneath a star of dazzling blue
Dazzling blue

Dazzling blue, roses red
Fine white linen to make a marriage bed
And we'll build a wall that nothing can break through
And dream our dreams of dazzling blue

Sweet July, and we drove the Montauk Highway
And walked along the cliffs above the sea
And we wondered why, and imagined it was someday
And that is how the future came to be

Dazzling blue, roses red
Fine white linen to make a marriage bed
And we'll build a wall that nothing can break through
And dream our dreams of dazzling blue

From the album *So Beautiful or So What*

373

Rewrite

I've been working on my rewrite, that's right
I'm gonna change the ending
Gonna throw away my title
And toss it in the trash
Every minute after midnight
All the time I'm spending
It's just for working on my rewrite
Gonna turn it into cash

I've been working at the Car Wash
I consider it my day job
'Cause it's really not a pay job
But that's where I am
Everybody says "The old guy
Working at the Car Wash
Hasn't got a brain cell left
Since Vietnam

But I say
Help me, help me
Help me, help me
Whoa! Thank you!
I'd no idea
That you were there

When I said help me, help me
Help me, help me
Thank you
For listening to my prayer

I'm working on my rewrite, that's right
I'm gonna change the ending
Gonna throw away my title
And toss it in the trash
Every minute after midnight

All the time I'm spending
Is just for working on my rewrite, that's right
I'm gonna turn it into cash
I'll eliminate the pages
Where the father has a breakdown
And he has to leave the family
But he really meant no harm
I'm gonna substitute a car chase
And a race across the rooftops
Where the father saves the children
And he holds them in his arms

And I say
Help me, help me
Help me, help me
Thank you!
I'd no idea
That you were there
When I said help me, help me
Help me, help me
Whoa! Thank you
For listening to my prayer

375

From the album *So Beautiful or So What*

Love and Hard Times

God and His only son
Paid a courtesy call on Earth
One Sunday morning
Orange blossoms opened their fragrant lips
Songbirds sang
From the tips of cottonwoods
Old folks wept
For His love in these hard times

"Well, we got to get going"
Said the restless Lord to the Son
"There are galaxies yet to be born
Creation is never done
Anyway, these people are slobs here
If we stay, it's bound to be a mob scene
But disappear, and it's love and hard times"

I loved her the first time I saw her
I know that's an old songwriting cliché
Loved you the first time I saw you
Can't describe it any other way
Any other way

The light of her beauty
Was warm as a summer day
Clouds of antelope rolled by
No hint of rain to come in the prairie sky
Just love, love, love, love, love

When the rains came
The tears burned
Windows rattled
Locks turned
It's easy to be generous
When you're on a roll

376

It's hard to be grateful
When you're out of control
And love is gone

The light at the edge of the curtain
Is the quiet dawn
The bedroom breathes in clicks and clacks
Uneasy heartbeat, can't relax
But then your hand takes mine
Thank God, I found you in time
Thank God, I found you
Thank God, I found you

From the album *So Beautiful or So What*

Love is eternal sacred light
Free from the shackles of time
Evil is darkness, sight without sight
A demon that feeds on the mind

How'd it all begin? Started with a bang
Couple of light years later, stars and planets sang
Fire warmed the cold, waves of colors flew
Moonlight into gold, Earth to green and blue

Love is eternal sacred light
Free from the shackles of time
Evil is darkness, sight without sight
A demon that feeds on the mind

Earth becomes a farm, farmer takes a wife
Wife becomes a river and the giver of life
Man becomes machine, oil runs down his face
Machine becomes a man with a bomb in the marketplace
Bomb in the marketplace, bomb in the marketplace

Love is eternal sacred light
Free from the shackles of time
Evil is darkness, sight without sight
A demon that feeds on the mind

Big Bang, that's a joke that I made up
Once when I had eons to kill
You know, most folks, they don't get when I'm joking
Well, maybe someday they will

Love me, love me
That's the main request I receive
Well, you know I love all my children
And it tears me up when I leave

But sometimes you gotta fly down that highway
Free as a bird, knock on wood, thank the Lord
I am driving along in my automobile
It's a brand-new pre-owned '96 Ford

Check out the radio, pop music station
That don't sound like my music to me
Talk show host, what's that boy's name?
Politics is ugly

At the end of the dial there's the gospel show
Maybe now I can exit and rest
There's a blizzard rolling down off the banks of Lake Michigan
Gonna cover the roads of the icy Midwest

Love is eternal sacred light
Free from the shackles of time
Evil is darkness, sight without sight
A demon that feeds on the mind

Love is eternal sacred light
Love is eternal sacred light
Love is eternal sacred light

379

From the album *So Beautiful or So What*

A pilgrim on a pilgrimage
Walked across the Brooklyn Bridge
His sneakers torn
In the hour when the homeless
Move their cardboard blankets
And the new day is born
Folded in his backpack pocket
The questions that he copied from his heart
Who am I in this lonely world?
And where will I make my bed tonight
When twilight turns to dark?

Questions for the angels
Who believes in angels?
Fools do
Fools and pilgrims all over the world

If you shop for love in a bargain store
And you don't get what you bargained for
Can you get your money back?
If an empty train in a railroad station
Calls you to its destination
Can you choose another track?
Will I wake up from these violent dreams
With my hair as white as the morning moon?

Questions for the angels
Who believes in angels?
I do
Fools and pilgrims all over the world
Downtown Brooklyn
The pilgrim is passing a billboard
That catches his eye
It's Jay-Z
He's got a kid on each knee

He's wearing clothes that he wants us to try
If every human on the planet
And all the buildings on it
Should disappear
Would a zebra grazing in the African Savannah
Care enough to shed one zebra tear?

Questions for the angels

From the album *So Beautiful or So What*

Love and blessings, simple kindness
Fell like rain on thirsty land
Fields and gardens, long abandoned
Came to life in dust and sand

Lover's lips sweet as honey
Touched as if old love was new
Banker's pockets overflowing with gold and money
Prophecies of wealth come true

Bop-bop-a-whoa
Ain't no song like an old song, Charlie
Bop-bop-a-whoa
There ain't no song like an old song, Charlie
Bop-bop-a-whoa
There ain't no time like a good time, Charlie
Bop-bop-a-whoa
Ain't no times like the good times, Charlie
Bop-bop-a-whoa
Whoa

Bop-bop-a-whoa
Bop-bop-a-whoa
Everywhere you look, anywhere you go
Everybody working for the
Bop-bop-a-whoa
Bop-bop-a-whoa
Bop-bop-a-whoa
Can't get enough of the
Bop-bop-a-whoa
Bop-bop-a-whoa
Bop-bop-a-whoa

If the summer kept a secret
It was heaven's lack of rain

Golden days and amber sunsets
Let the scientists complain

Came the autumn, drained of color
Ghosts in the water beg for more
Maple trees just a little bit duller
Than the memory of the year before

In a word, or in an image
Something called me from my sleep
Love and blessings, simple kindness
Ours to hold but not to keep

From the album *So Beautiful or So What*

383

I'm going to make a chicken gumbo
Toss some sausage in the pot
I'm going to flavor it with okra
Cayenne pepper to make it hot
You know life is what we make of it
So beautiful or so what

I'm going to tell my kids a bedtime story
A play without a plot
Will it have a happy ending?
Maybe yeah, maybe not
I tell them life is what you make of it
So beautiful or so what
So beautiful
So beautiful
So what

I'm just a raindrop in a bucket
A coin dropped in a slot
I am an empty house on Weed Street
Across the road from the vacant lot
You know life is what you make of it
So beautiful or so what

Ain't it strange the way we're ignorant
How we seek out bad advice
How we jigger it and figure it
Mistaking value for the price
And play a game with time and love
Like a pair of rolling dice
So beautiful
So beautiful
So what

Four men on the balcony
Overlooking the parking lot
Pointing at a figure in the distance
Dr. King has just been shot
And the Sirens' long melody
Singing "Savior, Pass Me Not"

Ain't it strange the way we're ignorant
How we seek out bad advice
How we jigger it and figure it
Mistaking value for the price
And play a game with time and love
Like a pair of rolling dice
So beautiful
So beautiful
So beautiful

From the album *So Beautiful or So What*

386

PUBLISHING INDEX

50 *Ways To Leave Your Lover* Copyright © 1975 by Paul Simon Music

The 59th Street Bridge Song (Feelin' Groovy) Copyright © 1966, 1994 by Paul Simon Music

7 *O'clock News/Silent Night* Copyright © 1966 by Paul Simon Music

Ace In The Hole Copyright © 1980 by Paul Simon Music

Adios Hermanos (with Derek Walcott) Copyright © 1997 by Paul Simon Music

The Afterlife © 2011 Words and Music by Paul Simon Paul Simon Music (BMI)

All Around the World or The Myth of Fingerprints Copyright © 1986 by Paul Simon Music

Allergies Copyright © 1981 by Paul Simon Music

America Copyright © 1968, 1996 by Paul Simon Music

American Tune Copyright © 1973, 1983 by Paul Simon Music

Another Galaxy (written by Paul Simon and Brian Eno) Copyright © 2006 by Paul Simon Music

April Come She Will Copyright © 1965, 1993 by Paul Simon Music

Armistice Day Copyright © 1968, 1996 by Paul Simon Music

At The Zoo Copyright © 1967, 1995 by Paul Simon Music

Baby Driver Copyright © 1969, 1997 by Paul Simon Music

Beautiful Copyright © 2006 by Paul Simon Music

Bernadette (with Derek Walcott) Copyright © 1997 by Paul Simon Music

The Big Bright Green Pleasure Machine Copyright © 1966, 1994 by Paul Simon Music

Bleecker Street Copyright © 1964 by Edward B. Marks Music Company

Blessed Copyright © 1966, 1994 by Paul Simon Music

Bookends Theme Copyright © 1968, 1996 by Paul Simon Music

Born at the Right Time Copyright © 1990 by Paul Simon Music

Born in Puerto Rico (with Derek Walcott) Copyright © 1997 by Paul Simon Music

The Boxer Copyright © 1968, 1996 by Paul Simon Music

The Boy in the Bubble (Words and music by Paul Simon and Forere Mothoeloa) Copyright © 1986 by Paul Simon Music

Bridge Over Troubled Water Copyright © 1969, 1997 by Paul Simon Music

Can I Forgive Him? (with Derek Walcott) Copyright © 1997 by Paul Simon Music

Can't Run But Copyright © 1990 by Paul Simon Music

Carlos & Yolanda (with Derek Walcott) Copyright © 1997 by Paul Simon Music